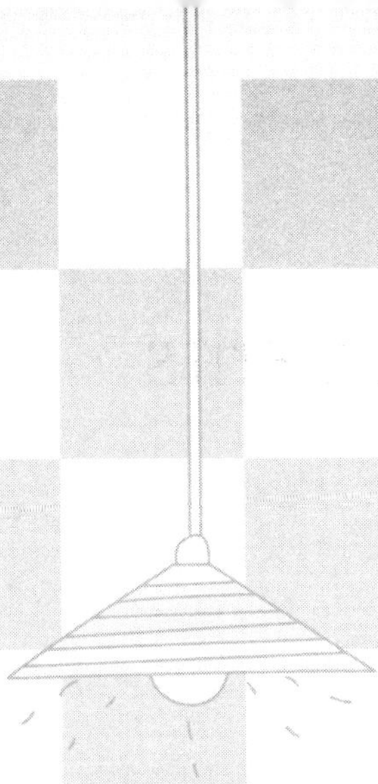

Guide to Kitchen English

Edited by **Kang, Kyung Jae**

"If you can imagine It, you can create it.
If you can describe it, you can fashion it.
If you can dream it, you can build it."

BAEKSAN Publishing Co

Preface & Acknowledgements

Guide to Kitchen English is the eighth book which I have developed since I served as an Professor, and it is the sixth book of Guide to series. When this book was first considered, my objective was to have a publication that would provide various contents to my students who major in Korean Cuisine, Chinese Cuisine, and Japanese Cuisine among 7 majors, Division of Hotel Culinary Arts & Foodservice to widen their views of culinary arts and to dig information about Foodservice world.

The title of this book is 'Guide to Kitchen English' which is named after Guide to Student Chef, published in 2001 that was the first book of Guide to series.

This book has a total of 4 parts which are Part 1 : Vocabulary, Part 2 : Expressions, Conversations, Idioms, Quizzes and Puzzles, Part 3 : Speaking, and Part 4 : Employment and Success. Each part has various chapters by the amount of material collected of each chapter. Each chapter has various sections by the degree of importance of the content and the amount of material collected of each chapter. In Chapter 1 Good Cooks and Word Facts, there are two sections which are Are you a good cook?, Word Facts. Chapter 2 Kitchen Utensils has two sections which cover Things found in the Kitchen, and Measuring Equipments. In Chapter 3 English Learning Materials for the Kitchen, there are two sections which deal with English Vocabulary for the Kitchen, and Questions about the Kitchen. Chapter 4 English Learning Materials for Food and Food-Related Things includes two sections which are Words used when talking about

Preface & Acknowledgements

the Food and Food-Related Things, and Questions about Food and Food-Related Words. In Chapter 5 Various Titles related to Chefs, there are three sections and you will explore Various Chef Titles in the Kitchen, Three Titles given to Kitchen Assistants, and Other Titles. Chapter 6 includes Culinary Verbs which has no section. In Chapter 7 Expressions used in The Kitchen there are Wait staff to Chef, Chef to Wait staff, and Among Kitchen Staff members. Chapter 8 Conversations about Food and Cooking has eight sections which provide you with A Chef's Life, How to be a Chef, Kitchen Safety, Recipe, Tacos, Veggies, Cooking Tips, and How to Make Spaghetti. In Chapter 9 Food Idioms, there are fifteen sections and you will learn Apple Idioms, Bean Idioms, Bread Idioms, Cake Idioms, Cooking Idioms, Drink Idioms, Egg Idioms, Fish Idioms, Fruit Idioms, Nut Idioms, Pie Idioms, Potato Idioms, Salt Idioms, Soup Idioms, and Stew Idioms. Chapter 10 True/ False Quizzes for Food Safety in the Kitchen has two sections which include Food Safety Quiz for Cold Food and Food Safety Quiz in Cooking. In Chapter 11 Crossword Puzzle and Word Puzzle there are three sections which prepare you for Kitchen Crossword, Restaurants and Food Crossword, and Kitchen Word Search. Chapter 12 Level one has nineteen sections which covers Greetings, Introduce Yourself, Introduce Kitchen Staff members, Identify People and Things, Ask for Information, Giving Information, Simple Sentences, Simple Questions, Number and Counting, Talking about company, Talking about Favourite Things, Talking about Here and Now, Talking about Feelings/Health Issues, Telling Time, Talking about Past

Actions, Talking about the Future (will vs. "be going to" + verb), Expressing Likes and Dislikes, Closing a Conversation, and Expressing Thanks. In Chapter 13 Level Two there are sixteen sections which examine American Numbers and Prices, Simple Shopping, Making Suggestions, Asking for Favors, Asking for Repetition, Requesting, Offering, Talking about Abilities, Expressing Possibility, Talking about Locations, Talking about Travel, Describing People and things, Like/Would like, Measure words, Telephone Talk, and Talking about Events during Lifelong Employment. Chapter 14 Level Three has nine sections and you will explore Giving Opinions, Asking for Details, Asking Permission, Asking for and Giving Advice, Sequencing, Discussing Sensitive Topics, Accepting and Refusing, Expressions for Descriptions, and Indirect Requests and Information Exchange. In Chapter 15 Level Four, there are thirteen sections which are Supporting Opinions, Exploring Options, Contrasting, Classifying, Discussion Techniques, Elaborating, Clarifying, Interrupting, Giving Instructions, Simple Presentations, Checking for Understanding, Conceding to Make a Point, and Analyzing Problems. Chapter 16 Level Five includes two sections which are Commenting Phrases for Conversation, and Paraphrasing Phrases for Conversation. Chapter 17 Examples of Career Opportunities show you two sections that are Career Opportunity for a Food service Company, and Career Opportunity for a Restaurant Group. In Chapter 18 Preparing for a Job Interview, there are two sections which covers Job interview questions interviewees hear, and Some things interviewees consider in advance.

Preface & Acknowledgements

Chapter 19 Job Interview Question and Answer English Tips has two sections which provide you with What is most important? and Talking about Responsibilities. Chapter 20 Examples for Lifelong Student and Continuing Education has four sections which show you ProChef Level II Success Story; Judy Doherty, ProChef Level III Success Story; Executive Chef, Steve Hickman, C.E.C., ProChef Level III Success Story; Chef Patrick Wilson, and ProChef Level II Success; Carol Murphy Clyne C.C.C. In Chapter 21 Introduction to Certified Master Chef, there is no section. Chapter 22 has two sections which show you President Ryan's Biography, and President Ryan's Career Snapshot. Each chapter has its own references at the end of the chapter. At the end of this book an appendix is added about Certified Master Chef Examination Manual.
I did major nothing relating to English Literature. This book is the eighth book among the books written by me and published before. For my students who are eager to become would-be professionals in this field, or the other field. I'm sure this book will act as an inspiration to always learn more, and encourage to gain confidence in studying English.

Eight years ago I was deeply impressed and shocked by the New Professional Chef 6th(ed.) which was given as a gift by one of my students, Mr. Yang, Kyu Mo. In the book there is a didactic sentence that can't be forgotten even in my dream that is "A true chef is, among other things, a lifelong student, a teacher, a craftsman, a leader, and a manager." The book has influenced tremendously and will influence me continuously. As the development of food and cuisine has never been completely one-sided, so culinary and foodservice education is not one-sided. Therefore students have to influence the persons engaging in culinary and foodservice education, and vice versa. I want to strongly emphasize that an interaction between students and the persons engaging in culinary and foodservice education is of great importance in culinary and foodservice education.

In writing this book I have already promised to myself more improved and updated book will be published in the next edition listing a body of information pertaining to culinary and foodservice.

I want to thank and acknowledge the following individuals for their help and assistance in the development of this book. The persons I have recognized here are some of those nice individuals from the food service industry who were willing to share their experiences, knowledge, and expertise.

My special thanks to: Professor Kim, Jong Young, Hyejeon College; Professor Cho'i Song San, Hyejeon College; Professor Kim, Yong Mun, Hyejeon College; Professor Kim, Kyung Im, Hyejeon College; Cho, Nam Kon, Director of Chonpok Myunka; Mun, Sung Kwon, Owner/Chef SamjungBonjum; Yeo, Kyung Rae, Predident of Hongbo Chinese Restaurant; Lee, Jong Wan President of WOORIM Japanese Restaurant; Yu, Dae Jun, President of KBTC(Korea Barista Training Center); Chong, Kyong Sung, Owner/Chef of Chonsu-sa Restaurant; Kim, Chun Hwi and

Preface & Acknowledgements

Ch'a Un Sim, Co-owner/Chef of Philadelphia Restaurant; Kwak, Jae Hun, Proprietor of OUTBACKSTEAKHOUSE; Yeo, Dae Sung, President of Bar oioi; Bae, In Ho, Chef, Millenium Hilton Hotel; Cho'i, Byung Uk, Team Manager of Elimsung Chinese Restaurant; Ryu, Si Ju, Team Manager of Sodo Food System Inc.; Kim, Young Bae, Team Manager of Foodvill Co., Ltd.; Seo, Sang Yun, Team Manager of F&B Division, Daemyung Leisure Industry Co., ltd.; Kim, Jong Ha, Team manager of Business Team, M Castle; Park, Chan Kuk, Team Manager of F&B Team.

I am grateful for the important materials provided by Yi, Kwang U, ex-my student of Department of Hotel Culinary Arts, Hyejeon College who works for Park Hyatt Hotel in Seoul.

I offer my thanks and gratitude to the below individuals for their help and assistance in the development of this edition.

My special thanks to: President Yi, Chae Ho, Hyejeon College; Vice President Yang, Chae Gil, FoodCulture of SAMSUNG EVERLAND INC.; Dr. Yun, Sung Ro, Yun's Surgical Clinic; Dr. Kim, Man Gil, Gil's Dermatological Clinic; Vice-General Manager Yu, Je Chun, Sheraton WalkerHill Hotel; Pedro Y.K. Yu, General Manager of Sales&Marketing, Lee Kum Kee Trading Ltd.; Fergus J. Han, Assitant Manager of Business Development, Lee Kum Kee Trading Ltd.; Chong, So In, Lee Kum Kee Trading Ltd.; Teacher Kim, Hang Sup, my close friend; Professor Shin, Sang Chun, Howon University; Professor Oh, Nam Sun, Kongju University; Professor Cho'i, Mun Gil, Hyejeon College; Professor Yu,

Kyong, Min, Chunch'on University; Professor Bae, Sang Mok, Hyejeon College; Professor Kim, Dong Ho, Hyejeon College; Professor Kang, Ch'ang Su, Hyejeon College; Professor Han, Min Su, Hyejeon College; Professor Yi, Yong Hwan, Hyejeon College; Professor Cho'i, Tae Ho, Hyejeon College; Professor Kim, Kyung Im, Hyejeon College; Preseident Cho, Byung Sook, Hongsung Cooking & Bakery School; Preseident Im, Kum Ran, Hwangje Food Academy;Preseident Yi, Young Ju, Seoch'on Cooking Academy; Vice-Preseident Chong, Hye Jung, Hongsung Cooking & Bakery School; Kim, Kyung Tae, Co-President of Hongju Funeral Service; Yi, Jun Seok, President of Kidjob Education Center; Yi, Sang In, Research Fellow of Kidjob Education Center; Kim, Young Su, Manager of Learning Center, Kookmin Bank; Park, Sang Hye, freelancer chef; wang, Sun Man, ex-teaching assistant of Department of Hotel Culinary Arts and FoodCulture of SAMSUNG EVERLAND INC.; Park, Ki Ho, ex-teaching assistant of Department of Hotel Culinary Arts, Hyejeon College; Oh, Ch'ol Hwan, graduate student of Graduate School of Kongju University; Yi, Hee Won, President Hotel; Yi, Sang Uk, Chef of Philadelphia Restaurant; Yeo, Woon Hyuk, Bakery of Grand Hyatt Seoul; Ka, Hui Chin, Cho, Hye Chin, Cho'i, Byung Ho, An Young Hye, Cho, Han pyo, teaching assistant of Hyejeon College; Yi, Bok Ku; Shin, Hyun Ok; Yi, Du Won; Ahn, Duk Kyun; Chon, Byong Wan; Cha'e Hui Duk; Yi, Ki Sun; Ji, Sung Jin; Cho'l, Tae Uk; Kim, Sang Jin; Heo, In Bum; Chu, Sung Un; Ham, Hye In; Kim, Nam Dong; Yi, Young Chun; Yi, Chong Won; Yang, In Kyu; Nam, Sung Hyun; Sung, Hyun Pil, Hyejeon

Preface & Acknowledgements

College.

I would like to thank my family, my wife Ko, Yon Suk, my first son, Kang, Byung Su(Bill), my only daughter, Kang, Dong Ok(Diana), and my second son, Kang, Duk(David) for their hard work, dedication, sacrifice, and assistance. I want to congratulate Bill on entering College of Oriental Medicine, Kyungwon University. Also I always thank for Bill, Diana, and David who are being grown up well and working very hard. Especially I want to appreciate my wife, Ko, Yon Suk, who has worked hard for our family, helping me with the manuscript and with a precious and invaluable dedication to accomplish a better publication. As a result I complete the development of this book.

God bless you!

Kang, Kyung Jae

Chairperson, Division of Hotel Culinary Arts and Foodservice,
Hyejeon College

Contents

Part 1 : Vocabulary

Part 2 : Expressions, Conversations, Idioms, Quizzes and Puzzles

Chapter 7 Expressions used in The Kitchen/85

Chapter 8 Conversations about Food and Cooking/92

Chapter 9 Food Idioms/110

Part 3 : Speaking

Chapter 12 Level one/145

Chapter 13 Level Two/160

Part 4 : Employment and Success

Chapter 17 Examples of Career Opportunities/209

Chapter 18 Preparing for a Job Interview/213

Chapter 19 Job Interview Question and Answer English Tips/219

Chapter 20 Examples for Lifelong Student and Continuing Education/227

Guide to Kitchen Enlgish

Part I

Vocabulary

Guide to Kitchen English

Chapter 1 Good Cooks and Word Facts

This chapter introduces you to a good cook, food, a recipe, and ingredients. These words are the basic ones you can think of when you begin cooking dishes as a cook in the kitchen.

1. Are you a good cook?

Would you say that you are a good cook? And how would you describe a good cook, and what makes a good cook? You think fundamentally someone who loves food and is interested in quality food and is interested in what happens when you prepare it, and somebody who wants to create food for other people. It's a fundamental life skill and it's a very caring and sharing thing to be able to do, whether you do it alone for other people or whether you cook, you know, with a number of other individuals. You think a good cook is somebody who is quite sensitive about flavour, taste, and texture of food. Really likes to produce something out of more inexpensive ingredients. It's not all about the most expensive foods that you can buy.

Let's move on to word facts.

2. Word Facts

1) Word Fact 1

Our first word today is Food—four letters, three sounds, one syllable. Food is what we eat. Food is a noun and appears in a number of phrases and expressions, not all of which are connected with eating.

You can buy food in a food-hall and prepare it using a food-processor. You have to cook it carefully because you don't want to get food-poisoning. The food-chain is a term in science to describe the natural system where one living thing is eaten by another.

It's important to try and keep chemicals out of the human food chain. That's why farmers can't use some medicines on their cattle.

Small creatures like insects are at the bottom of the food chain. Large animals like humans are at the top of the food chain. But the food-chain can also be a humorous expression to describe your position in a company.

You've just started here so you're at the bottom of the food chain. But you hope you can work your way up in a few years.

Another expression using food is when something makes you think carefully about a particular subject. It gives you food for thought.

2) Word Fact 2

Our next word is recipe. R E - C - I - P - E. Recipe. It has three syllables with the stress on the first syllable. A recipe is the set of instructions for how to make a particular food. It often goes together with the verb 'to follow'

You think it's very important to follow recipes precisely. It's the only way to know what you will get!

The preposition which is used with recipe is 'for', but it usually not stressed and sounds like / f. /

Do you know a good recipe for chicken soup? To be a recipe for something is also an expression for something that is very likely to happen.

One of the most common phrases like this is 'a recipe for disaster'. Leaving your greedy dog in the same room as your freshly made cake is a recipe for disaster!

3) Word Fact 3

Our next word is the noun 'ingredient' - i – n – g – r – e –d – i –e – n – t. The plural is regular, you add an 's' , ingredients, but notice that the 't' at the end of the word becomes silent. It's not pronounced. Ingredients are the different things that go together to make a meal. You always try to use the freshest ingredients when cooking. A cheese omelette doesn't have many ingredients. Just eggs and cheese, and maybe salt and pepper if you like. Ingredient is also used for something that is very important to making something effective. It often goes together with adjectives essential, vital or important. Good communication is an essential ingredient of a successful relationship.

N.o.t.e

–**caring** : compassionate or showing concern for others

–**syllable** : a unit of spoken language that consists of one or more vowel sounds alone, a syllabic consonant alone, or any of these with one or more consonant sounds

–**food–hall** : a place to buy local fresh, seasonal food at its very best

–**greedy** : wanting a lot more food, money, etc. than you need

R.e.f.e.r.n.c.e.s

http://downloads.bbc.co.uk/worldservice/learningenglish/webcast/scripts/tae_wc_cooking_070621.pdf

http://dictionary.cambridge.org/

http://en.wikipedia.org/wiki/

http://encarta.msn.com/encnet/features/dictionary/

http://www.merriam-webster.com/

http://www.onelook.com/

Chapter 2 Kitchen Utensils

This chapter introduces you to basic tools and equipment referred to as kitchen utensils which are used during food preparation, cooking and serving. You cannot start your business without these tools and equipment. So, you should be able to identify and use the tools and equipment for the specific jobs in the business. These tools and equipment increase efficiency of your jobs and save time.

1. Things found in the Kitchen

You can put these tools and equipment into groups according to their sizes and functions. But in this chapter for convenience's sake they are classified as large, small and mechanical equipment like our college does.

1) Large equipment

These equipment or items can be put under this group, which are big and sometimes fixed :

broilers, broom cupboards, closets (cupboards/cabinets), cooking ranges, countertops (worktop/cooktop/work surface), dish washers, draining board, fridge(or refrigerators), fridge- freezers, fryers, ice machines, microwave (ovens), ovens, salamanders, sinks,
washing up bowl(or washing basins), washing machines, working tables,

2) Small equipment

Sometimes these are classified as tools which are also referred to as small cooking utensils. They are small and easy to carry about. Let's list all the tools on this group :

chef's knives (sometimes referred to as utility knives), slicing knives,
paring knives, butcher (carving) knives, butter knives,
tin openers, bottle opener, spoons of all kinds and sizes,
pestle and mortar, colanders, sieves, strainers, kitchen scales,
serving dishes of all kinds and sizes, jars, jugs, cups,
funnels, kettles, kitchen scissors(shears), tongs,
kitchen forks, ladles, lemon squeezer,
measuring spoons(teaspoon, dessert spoon and table spoon),
measuring cups, scoops, sifters, mixing bowl,
saucepans (different sizes), rolling pin, peelers,
frying pans(shallow frying pans, deep frying pans, woks), casseroles,
shredder or grater, cutting boards/chopping boards,
thermometer, spatulas, dishpans,
baking sheets (baking trays/baking tins), chopsticks, corkscrews,
mug, bread bins, ironing boards, ice cube trays,
mops, buckets, roasting tins,
aluminium foil (metal paper), cling film (thin plastic wrap),
freezer bags, skimmers,

3) Mechanical equipment.

These are referred to as appliances, which are operated by electricity and are classified as mechanical equipment :

mixers, liquidizers (blenders/food processors), slicers,
mincers, electric kettles, rice cookers,
pressure cookers, toasters, coffee makers, yogurt makers,
cafetiere, cookers/grills, teapots, coffee grinders, stoves,

N.o.t.e

-utensil : a tool with a particular use, especially in a kitchen or house

-broom : a brush with a long handle, used for cleaning the floor
-closet : a cupboard or a small room with a door, used for storing things, especially clothes

-draining board : a sloping grooved surface on which crockery is left to drain into an adjacent sink.

-fridge (ALSO refrigerator, US OLD-FASHIONED ice-box) : a piece of kitchen equipment which uses electricity to preserve food at a cold temperature

-fridge- freezer : a piece of kitchen equipment divided into two parts for preserving food, one of which is a fridge and the other a freezer
-oven : the part of a cooker with a door, which is used to cook food

-salamander : A salamander is a huge commercial grill that can be heated to very high temperatures. It's used by professional cooks for glazing, browning or caramelising savoury or sweet dishes.

-washing basin : a basin in which to wash one's face and hands

-pestle and mortar : a heavy stick made of clay, stone or metal, with a thick rounded end, which is used for crushing substances in a mortar (= a small strong bowl) by hitting or rubbing them

-colander : a bowl with small holes in it which is used for washing food or for emptying food into when it has been cooked in water ex) After four minutes, pour the pasta into a colander to drain.

-sieve : a tool consisting of a wood, plastic or metal frame with a wire or plastic net fixed to it. You use it either to separate solids from a liquid, or you rub larger solids through it to make them smaller ex) Pass the sauce through a sieve to remove any lumps.

N.o.t.e

–**strainer** : a device, usually incorporating a mesh or other filter, for separating solids from liquids or small particles from large

–**funnel** : an object which has a wide round opening at the top, sloping sides, and a narrow tube at the bottom, used for pouring liquids or powders into containers with narrow necks

–**sifter** : a container with many small holes in its lid for sifting powdery substances, usually foods

–**baking sheet** : a flat metal dish used to cook things in an oven -dishpan : A flat-bottomed basin for washing dishes.

–**corkscrew** : a device for removing corks from bottles, which consists of a handle with a twisted metal rod to screw into the cork and pull it out

–**baking tin** : A baking tin is a metal container used for baking things such as cakes and bread in an oven.

–**bread bin** : a container used to keep bread or cake in

–**roasting tin** : A deep-sided metal container, usually rectangular in shape, for roasting meat, poultry or vegetables.

–**cling film** : a thin clinging transparent plastic film used as a wrapping or covering for food.

–**appliance** : a device, machine or piece of equipment, especially an electrical one that is used in the house such as a cooker or washing machine

–**liquidizer** : UK FOR blender (= electric machine that changes food into a thick liquid)

–**cafetiere** : a glass container for making coffee, in which hot water is poured onto coffee and then a filter (= net) is pushed down into the container to keep the solids at the bottom.

2. Measuring Equipments

These are classified as small equipment, but in a professional kitchen they are considered as essential equipment. Common measurements taken in a kitchen are weight, volume, temperature and size. Measurements are determined in many different ways, depending upon the ingredient to be measured and the system employed by the specific recipes. It is important to have equipment for liquid and dry volume measures for both US and metric, as well as a variety of scales for accurate measurement by weight. Thermometers should display both Fahrenheit and Centigrade temperatures.

1) Scales

Most recipe ingredients are measured by weight, so accurate scales are very important. Portion scales are used for measuring ingredients as well as for portioning products for service.

2) Graduated Measuring Pitchers (Volume measures)

These are used for measuring liquids and are generally available in pint, quart, half gallons and gallon sizes. Each size is marked off into fourths by ridges on the sides.

3) Measuring Cups

These are available in 1, 1/2, 1/3, and 1/4 cup sizes. They can be used for both liquid and dry measures.

4) Measuring Spoons

These are used for measuring very small volumes: 1 tablespoon, 1 teaspoon, $\frac{1}{2}$ teaspoon, and $\frac{1}{4}$ teaspoon. They are used most often for spices and seasonings.

5) Ladles

These are sued for measuring and portioning liquids. The size, in ounces, is stamped on the handle.

6) Scoops

These come in standard sizes and have a lever for mechanical release. They are used for portioning soft solid foods. The number of the scoop indicates the number of level scoopfuls per quart. In actual use a rounded scoopful is often more practical, so exact weights will vary.

7) Thermometers

These measure temperatures. There are many kinds for many purposes:

① A meat thermometer indicates internal temperature of meats. It is inserted before cooking and left in the product during cooking.

② An instant-read thermometer will give readings within a few seconds of being inserted in a food product. It reads from 0 to 220°F. Many chefs carry these in their jacket pockets like a pen, ready whenever needed. Instant-read thermometers must not be left in meats during roasting, or they will be damaged.

③ Fat thermometers and candy thermometers test temperatures of frying fats and sugar syrups. They read up to 400°F.

④ Probe Thermometer : Food hygiene testing instrument to test foods from cold to hot foods out from temperature danger zone (tdz).

⑤ Special thermometers are used to test the accuracy of oven, refrigerator, and freezer thermostats.

N.o.t.e

- **Scales** : (US scale) a device for weighing things or people
- **Graduated** : divided into levels or stages
- **Pitcher** : UK a large container with a wide round base, straight sides and a narrow opening at the top, used in the past for holding water or another liquid
- **mark off** : to separate one area from another by means of a boundary line or barrier
- **ridge** : a long narrow raised area of something
- **come in** : to arrive or be received and become available for use, sale, or communication
- **lever** : a bar or handle which moves around a fixed point, so that one end of it can be pushed or pulled in order to control the operation of a machine or move a heavy or stiff object
- **release** : to take the tension off a mechanism such as a spring, brake, or catch and so allow something to move, open, or operate
- **temperature danger zone** : Temperature danger zone is 40° to 140°F (4.4° to 60°C). Cooked, ready to eat food should not be left in the temperature danger zone for any longer than necessary. If it has been in the zone less than two hours, it can be refrigerated or used immediately.
- **thermostat** : a device that controls the temperature of a system by automatically switching the supply of heat or cool air on and off when the temperature becomes too cool or too hot

R.e.f.e.r.n.c.e.s

http://www.asianspicyrecipes.com/measuring_equipments.php

http://dictionary.cambridge.org/

http://en.wikipedia.org/wiki/

http://encarta.msn.com/encnet/features/dictionary/

http://www.merriam-webster.com/

http://www.onelook.com/

Chapter 3 English Learning Materials for the Kitchen

1. English Vocabulary for the Kitchen.

This passage is about English vocabulary for the kitchen. You can pick up about 50 kitchen related words reading this passage. Let's read English vocabulary for the kitchen.

Some people have a fitted kitchen, where all the kitchen units have been bought together, and they are assembled according to a plan. Other people have a kitchen where the units are free-standing: not necessarily bought together at one time.

In a kitchen you are likely to find cupboards (or cabinets), either at floor level, or at eye level. In the eye level cupboards you will probably find dry goods (such as flour, sugar, rice, pasta, spices) and maybe glasses and crockery (plates, bowls etc). In the floor level cupboards you might find pots and pans: saucepans for cooking pasta etc; frying pans for frying food; baking tins and roasting tins for cooking food in the oven; and serving dishes made from glass or china. You could also find other kitchen implements such as a blender (= food processor) and kitchen scales (for measuring and weighing food). Often the top part of a floor level cupboard has a drawer, where various items are kept, such as cutlery (knives, forks and spoons); aluminium foil (metal paper), cling film (thin plastic wrap), freezer bags, and other kitchen items such as a bread knife, tin opener, corkscrew (to open bottles of wine), potato peeler (to take the skin off potatoes), a rolling pin (to roll out pastry) and so on.

On the top of the floor level cupboards you often find a worktop or work surface, where you can prepare food. These surfaces are sometimes made of marble, or hard wood, and thcy can be easily cleaned. Some people keep a toaster or microwave on the work surfaces, along with things they need frequently, such as oil, salt, or various sauces.

Most kitchens also contain a cooker with an oven and four rings, (although some modern cookers are split level, where the oven is separate from the rings), a fridge-freezer, and perhaps a dishwasher or even a washing machine. You'll probably find a kitchen sink, where you wash the plates and dishes, and larger kitchens also contain a kitchen table and chairs, so you can eat in the same room.

N.o.t.e

–**crockery** : cups, plates, bowls, etc., used to serve food and drink, especially made of china

–**cutlery** : knives, forks and spoons used for eating food

–**marble** : a type of very hard rock which has a pattern of lines going through it, feels cold and becomes smooth and shiny when cut and polished

–**ring** : a circular piece of material often made of metal that can be heated in order to be used for cooking

2. Questions about the Kitchen

Below are various questions about things found in the kitchen. Through various questions you are able to learn the names and uses of things found in the kitchen.

1) Where can I find a _______ ?

Where do you put the kitchen utensils? Put the objects below in the correct drawer or cupboard:

a. In the drawer with the cutlery (forks, for example).

b. In the cupboard with the crockery (plates, for example).

c. In the cupboard with the large cooking utensils(saucepans, for example).

a wok, a bowl, a frying pan, a saucer, a corkscrew, a cup, a teaspoon, a tin opener, a mug, hopsticks, a dish, spoons, a casserole dish, knives, a serving spoon, a baking tray, a bottle opener

Drawer a	Cupboard b	Cupboard c

2) Match the words

Match some of the words above with the definitions below.

a. You use it to open wine bottles.

b. You use it to open beer bottles.

c. You use it to cook Chinese food.

d. You use it to bake cakes.

Which is usually deeper - a bowl or a dish?

Which is usually bigger - a mug or a cup?

3) Match the words

Match the kitchen job to the thing you use to do it.

Boil water	oven gloves
Wash the dishes	kettle
Wipe the kitchen table	tea towel
Dry the dishes	dish cloth
Wash the kitchen floor	wooden spoon
Stir the sauce	washing up liquid
Take the roast chicken out of the oven	mop

4) Read and Match

Read the description of the kitchen and look at the underlined words.

My kitchen is light and airy with bright yellow walls and lots of cupboards and shelves. There is a big fridge freezer in the corner covered in post-it notes and fridge magnets, and there is a washing machine and a dishwasher in the alcove at the back of the room. I have a lovely long work surface made of beech with lots of useful gadgets on it: a toaster, a teapot, a cafeiere, a kettle, and a food processor. There is also a chopping board and a bread bin. The cooker is brand new, with a grill, and an oven big enough to take a Christmas turkey. On the other side of the kitchen, beneath a window that overlooks the garden, the sink and draining board are made of stainless steel. There is a washing up bowl in the sink of course, and next to the sink there is a broom cupboard which is full of mops and buckets and an ironing board. Finally, tucked away in the corner, is the microwave, which, if I'm honest, is the thing that gets used most often in my kitchen.

Which of the underlined words in the text are needed to do the jobs in the list below? Which job can't be done in this kitchen?

- Tidy the pots and pans away
- Tidy the brushes and mops away
- Keep things cool
- Wash dishes
- Wash dishes mechanically
- Make coffee
- Keep bread fresh
- Grill meat
- Freeze food

- Grind coffee
- Boil water
- Make toast
- Mix food to make sauces
- Wash clothes
- Prepare food
- Roast meat
- Reheat food quickly
- Make tea
- Iron clothes

5) Fill in the blanks in these sentences with words from the box.

refrigerator, paring knife, microwave (oven), ice cube trays, mop, bucket, closet, ingredients, butcher (carving) knife, frying pan, toaster, dishwasher, stove, freezer, butter knife, cupboard, pan

① Ted filled the _________ with water and put them in the _____ so they would be ready when she made iced tea.

② The cook began frying eggs in the _________ and put two slices of bread in the _________.

③ Jack loaded the dirty dishes into the _________.

④ Jill put the clean dishes in the ___________.

⑤ People use a ___________ to heat food quickly.

⑥ Betty wanted to bake a cake, but she did not have all of the _________.

⑦ Mother put the milk and eggs she just bought in the _______ to keep them fresh.

⑧ You use a _______ to peel potatoes, a _______ to slice a turkey, and a ________________ to spread peanut butter.

⑨ Donna put soup in the ________ and placed it on the ______ to heat.

⑩ Mrs. Jones took the ________ and ________ from the _____ to clean the muddy kitchen floor.

6) Paraphrasing

These are things found in the kitchen. Find the correct word from the box.

fridge, bowl, flour, whisk, sink, yoghurt, oven, butter, spice

① a type of powder or seed (used to give flavour to food) -

② soft yellow fat made from cream or milk -

③ part of a cooker with a door -

④ thick liquid food prepared from milk (bacteria are added to it) -

⑤ a basin in the kitchen (connected to the water supply) -

⑥ an instrument for stirring eggs -

⑦ white or brown powder (used for making bread and cake) -

⑧ a round container open at the top -

⑨ a chamber in which food is kept cold - fridge

N.o.t.e

-post-it(note) : a small coloured piece of paper for short messages which can be stuck temporarily to something else

-alcove : a small space in a room, formed by one part of a wall being further back than the parts on each side

-beech : a tree with a smooth grey trunk and small nuts, or the wood from this tree

-be tucked away/along, etc. to be in a place which is hidden or where few people go

-load : to put a lot of things into a vehicle or machine

-Paraphrase : to repeat something written or spoken using different words, often in a humorous form or in a simpler and shorter form that makes the original meaning clearer

Answers

1

a. In the drawer with the cutlery (forks, for example): a corkscrew, a teaspoon, a tin opener, chopsticks, a bottle opener, spoons, knives, a serving spoon

b. In the cupboard with the crockery (plates, for example): a bowl, a saucer, a cup, a mug, a dish, a casserole dish

c. In the cupboard with the large cooking utensils (saucepans, for example): a wok, a frying pan, a baking tray

2

a. corkscrew, b. bottle opener, c. wok, d. baking tray

Which is usually deeper? - a bowl

Which is usually bigger? - a mug

3

Boil water - kettle

Wash the dishes - washing up liquid

Wipe the kitchen table - dish cloth

Dry the dishes - tea towel

Wash the kitchen floor - mop

Stir the sauce - wooden spoon

Take the roast chicken out of the oven - oven gloves

4

Tidy the pots and pans away - cupboards

Tidy the brushes and mops away - broom cupboard

Keep things cool - fridge freezer

Wash dishes - sink/draining board/washing up bowl

Wash dishes mechanically - dishwasher

Make coffee - cafetiere

Keep bread fresh - bread bin

Grill meat - cooker/grill

Freeze food - fridge freezer

Boil water - kettle

Make toast - toaster

Mix food to make sauces - food processor

Wash clothes - washing machine

Prepare food - chopping board

Roast meat - cooker/oven

Reheat food quickly - microwave

Make tea - teapot

Iron clothes - ironing board

Grind coffee is the job that can't be done. You need a coffee grinder.

5

① ice cube trays, freezer, ② frying pan, toaster, ③ dishwasher,

④ cupboard ⑤ microwave (oven) ⑥ ingredients,

⑦ refrigerator ⑧ paring knife, butcher (carving) knife, butter knife,

⑨ pan, stove, ⑩ mop, bucket, closet

6

① spice ② butter ③ oven ④ yoghurt ⑤ sink

⑥ whisk ⑦ flour ⑧ bowl ⑨ fridge

R.e.f.e.r.n.c.e.s

http://www.onestopenglish.com/section.asp?docid=147102

http://www.englisch-hilfen.de/en/exercises/kitchen1.htm

http://www.english-at-home.com/vocabulary/english-vocabulary-for-the-kitchen/

http://www.cooking4chumps.com/Lingo%20Kitchen%20Vocabulary%20Language.html

http://www.english-at-home.com/vocabulary/english-vocabulary-for-the-kitchen/

http://www.cooking4chumps.com/Lingo%20Kitchen%20Vocabulary%20Language.html

http://dictionary.cambridge.org/

http://en.wikipedia.org/wiki/

http://encarta.msn.com/encnet/features/dictionary/

http://www.merriam-webster.com/

http://www.onelook.com/

Chapter 4 English Learning Materials for Food and Food-Related Things

1. Words used when talking about the Food and Food-Related Things

The words below are some of the most important used when talking about the food and food-related things. They are also instrumental to describe something about the food and food-related things. If possible you should memorize them.

1) Condition : fresh, off, past its sell-by date, raw, ripe, rotten , tough, undercooked, unripe, overcooked
2) Quantities : bar, liter, loaf, lump, piece, pint, portion, slice, spoonful, handful(See Chapter 14)
3) Taste : bitter, bland, creamy, crisp, crunchy, hot, mild, salty, savory, sickly, sour, spicy, stodgy, sweet, tasteless
4) Types : barbecue, buffet, four-course meal, picnic, snack, TV dinner
5) Eating and Drinking : bite, chew, swallow, sip
6) Preparing : add, fill, mix, pour, shake, stir etc. (See Chapter 22)
7) Other Related Words : crumbs, fast food, (non)-fattening, helping, pastry, slimming, sticky

2. Questions about Food and Food-Related Words

Below are various questions about food and food-related words. Through various questions you are able to learn the meanings of food and food-related words.

1) Choose the one word or phrase that best completes the sentence.

① Lemons taste _________.

a. salty b. sour c. bitter d. crunchy e. bland

② Potato chips are not _________.

a. crisp b. salty c. crunchy d. juicy e. junk food

③ Smooth foods don't include _________.

a. crackers b. ice cream c. pudding d. whipped cream e. avocado

④ In a restaurant, we normally eat an appetizer _________.

a. after the entree
b. just before dessert
c. first
d. last
e. only if we are not very hungry

⑤ If something is filling it is _______________ .

a. the stuff inside a pie
b. something that you eat, but you are still hungry
c. delicious
d. something that you eat and you feel full after eating it
e. both a and d

⑥ Finger food ________.

a. makes your fingernails grow longer
b. is only in eaten in countries where they don't have silverware
c. is slang for a bad gesture
d. is food you can politely eat with your hands
e. is the name of a really tasty candy bar

⑦ Light food is the opposite of ________.

a. heavy food b. rich food c. bland food
d. junk food e. health food

⑧ If something is tasty, you ________.

a. don't really enjoy eating it
b. think it tastes good
c. hate eating it
d. only eat it for breakfast
e. think it is unappetizing

⑨ Spicy food includes ________.

a. milk b. lemons c. chili peppers d. bananas e. hamburgers

⑩ If milk is sour it is ________.

a. delicious b. too old c. too fresh d. from a goat e. from a coconut

⑪ A beverage is ________.

a. Beverley's birthday
b. something red
c. an alcoholic drink
d. any drink
e. normally crunchy

⑫ All of these are bitter except ________.

a. black coffee
b. strong tea without sugar or milk
c. unsweetened baking chocolate
d. pizza
e. a and c

⑬ Appetizing means _________.

a. you would like to eat it
b. the first course at a restaurant
c. yucky
d. tangy
e. finger food

⑭ Sweet foods don't include _________.

a. cake b. pickles c. ice cream d. candy e. strawberries

⑮ Rich food is always _________.

a. salty b. crunchy c. dessert d. fattening e. expensive

2) Choose the correct word from the box.

sour, sweet, bitter, succulent, starve, moist, thirsty, rich, dry, full

① A lemon or an unripe apple tastes ________ .

② After eating a lot or when something can't have more put in it, we say _______.

③ What word means not having enough water, liquid, or moisture?

④ This word is most often heard when talking of wealth. When a cake or sauce contains a lot of dairy products such as butter, cream or eggs we say it is _______.

⑤ When a person wants a drink they are ________.

⑥ What word is used favourably about cakes and bread and is the opposite of dry?

⑦ The real meaning of this word is to die or suffer from hunger, but we use it colloquially to describe being hungry. This word is ________ .

⑧ A word used when talking about fruit or meat that means it is juicy and tastes good is   .

⑨ Something that taste like unsweetened cocoa or beer is said to be __________.

⑩ The opposite of sour and means that something tastes of sugar or honey is ___________.

N.o.t.e

- **instrumental** : serving as a means of pursuing an aim
- **off** : (of food and drink) no longer fresh or good to eat because of being too old
- **sell-by date** : a date displayed on food and pharmaceutical products, after which they should not be sold
- **bland** : lacking a strong taste or character or lacking in interest or energy
- **crunchy** : describes food that is firm and makes a loud noise when it is eaten
- **savory** : ①having an appetizing taste or smell, ②salty or sharp-tasting rather than sweet
- **sickly** : provoking feelings of disgust or nausea
- **spicy** : containing strong flavours from spice
- **stodgy** : describes food which is heavy and unhealthy, sometimes in an unpleasant way
- **crumb** : a very small piece of bread, cake or biscuit
- **fattening** : describes food that contains a lot of fat, sugar, etc. that would quickly make you fatter if you ate a lot of it
- **helping** : an amount of food given to one person at one time
- **slimming** : used for losing weight or intended to help with losing weight
- **sticky** : having adhesive qualities
- **yucky** : disgusting or unpleasant
- **tangy** : A tangy flavour is pleasantly strong and sharp
- **succulent** : (of food) tender, juicy, and tasty
- **colloquial** : (of words and expressions) informal and more suitable for use in speech than in writing

Answers

1

① b ② d ③ a ④ c ⑤ e ⑥ d ⑦ a ⑧ b

⑨ c ⑩ b ⑪ d ⑫ d ⑬ a ⑭ b ⑮ d

2

① sour ② full ③ dry ④ rich ⑤ thirsty ⑥ moist

⑦ starve ⑧ succulent ⑨ bitter ⑩ sweet

R.e.f.e.r.n.c.e.s

http://downloads.bbc.co.uk/worldservice/learningenglish/webcast/scripts/tae_wc_cooking_quiz_070628.pdf

http://a4esl.org/q/h/vc-food-lb.html

http://www.englishclub.com/english-for-work/food-drink-back.htm

http://a4esl.org/q/h/0001/bh-food.html

http://esl.about.com/library/vocabulary/blwordgroups_food.htm

http://esl.about.com/library/vocabulary/blwordgroups_food.htm

http://www.englishclub.com/english-for-work/food-drink-back.htm

http://dictionary.cambridge.org/

http://en.wikipedia.org/wiki/

http://encarta.msn.com/encnet/features/dictionary/

http://www.merriam-webster.com/

http://www.onelook.com/

Chapter 5 Various Titles related to Chefs

1. Various Chef Titles in the Kitchen

Below are various titles given to those working in a professional kitchen and each can be considered a title for a type of chef. Many of the titles are based on the brigade system documented by Georges Auguste Escoffier. Specialized and hierarchial chef titles are usually found only in fine-dining, upscale restaurants; kitchen staff members at casual restaurants such as diners may be called chefs but are more often called "cook" or ,"short-order cook".

What does Executive chef do?

This person is in charge of everything related to the kitchen, including menu creation, staff management and business aspects. While the position requires extensive cooking experience and often involves actively cooking, it also involves a high level of management and business aspects of the kitchen. They can also be referred to as the "chef" or "head chef".

What is Chef de Cuisine (Chief of the Kitchen)?

It is a synonym for the title executive chef. In some establishments this title is used to designate a chef who is the head chef at one location of an operation that has multiple locations where the corporate chef has the title executive chef.

What does Sous chef do?

This person is the direct assistant of the executive chef and is second in command. It may be responsible for scheduling, and filling in for the executive chef when they are off-duty. It also will fill in or assist the chef de partie (line cooks) when needed.

What does Expediter(=Announcer) (Aboyeur) do?

This person takes the orders from the dining room and relays them to the stations in the kitchen. This person also often puts the finishing touches on the dish before it goes to the dining room.

What is Chef de Partie?

It is also called as a "station chef" or "line cook", and in charge of the kitchen's production area. In large kitchens line cooks are often divided into a hierarchy of their own, starting with "First Cook", then "Second Cook", and so on as needed.

Below are various hierarchial chef titles which are under the control of station chef in the brigade system. Let's look at these titles further.

What is Sauté Chef (Saucier)?

This person is responsible for all sautéed items and their sauce. This is usually the highest position of all the stations.

What does Fish Chef (Poissonier) do?

This person is in charge of fish dishes and often does all fish butchering as well as appropriate sauce. This station may be combined with the saucier position.

What does Roast Chef (Rotisseur) do?

This person prepares roasted and braised meats and their appropriate sauce.

What does Grill Chef (Grillardin) do?

This person takes care of all grilled foods. This position may be combined with the rotisseur.

What does Fry Chef (Friturier) do?

This person has charge of all fried items. It may be combined with the rotisseur position.

What does Vegetable Chef (Entremetier) do?

This person has charge of hot appetizers and often prepares the soups, vegetables, pastas and starches. Meanwhile, In a full brigade system this can be further divided into potager(soup cook) and a legumier (vegetable cook).

What is Roundsman (Tournant)?

This person is also referred to as a swing cook and relief cook, and fills in as needed on station in kitchen.

What is Pantry Chef (Garde Manger)?

This person is responsible for preparing cold foods, including salads, cold appetizers, pâtés and other charcuterie items.

What does Butcher (Boucher) do?

This person prepares butchers meats, poultry and sometimes fish. It may also be responsible for breading meats and fish.

What does Pastry Chef (Pâtissier) do?

This person prepares baked goods, pastries and desserts. In larger establishments, the pastry chef often supervises a separate team in their own kitchen or separate shop. Some kitchens may have an executive pastry chef.

2. Three Titles given to Kitchen Assistants

What does Apprentice (Commis) do?

This person works under a chef de partie (station chef) in order to learn the station's responsibilities and operation.

What is Communard?

This person is in charge of preparing the meal for the staff during a shift. This meal is often referred to as family meal.

What is Dishwasher (escuelerie)?

This person is the keeper of dishes, having charge of dishes and keeping the kitchen clean.

3. Other Titles

Due to the explosion of cooking shows on the TV and other media, here are other titles associated with Chefs.

What is Celebrity Chef?

This is a person who become famous because of his cooking, but it is also tagged as a negative thing for a chef who has “sold out” or gone mainstream to the media. Many consider Antoine Careme as the first celebrity chef and other popular chefs includes Rachel Ray and Jeff “The Frugal Chef, Smith.

What is Iron Chef?

Iron Chef is a Japanese television program produced by FujiTV. The original Japanese title is Ironmen of Cooking. We can mention 4 Iron Chefs who are Mario Batali, Cat Cora, Bobby Flay, and Masaharu Morimoto. Mario Batali specializes in Italian cuisine, Cat Cora is the first female Iron Chef and a Greek and Aegean cuisine specialist, Bobby Flay specializes in Southwestern Cuisine, and Masaharu Morimoto specializes in neo-Japanese cuisine.

What is Personal Chef?

This person goes to a client's home to prepare meals for the client based on their needs and wants. His/Her duties includes making the menu and budget, purchasing the ingredients, preparing the meal, and cleaning up after the preparation.

N.o.t.e

–brigade : a large group of soldiers in an army
-document : to record the details of an event, a process, etc

–hierarchy : a system in which people or things are arranged according to their importance

–upmarket(MAINLY US upscale) : describes goods and products that are of very high quality and intended to be bought by people who are quite rich

–diners : MAINLY US a small restaurant at the side of the road

–synonym : a word or phrase which has the same or nearly the same meaning as another word or phrase in the same language

–designate : to state officially that a place or thing has a particular character or purpose

–fill in (REPLACE) : to do someone else's work for them because they cannot or will not do it themselves

-charcuterie : It is a generic term for the products traditionally sold by charcutiers (pork butchers), and includes all products based on pork meat or offal, including cured and cooked meats, fresh and smoked sausages, pâtés, black puddings and salamis. It also refers to the shop itself that sells these kinds of products. Order charcuterie in a restaurant and you'll be served a platter of cuts of meats and sausages prepared in various ways.

–tag : to attach or give an epithet to; label.

–sell out(SELL BUSINESS) : to sell your business or part of your business

–mainstream : the way of life or set of beliefs accepted by most people

–Aegean : of or relating to or bordering the Aegean Sea

–neo– : new or recent, or in a modern form

R.e.f.e.r.n.c.e.s

http://dictionary.cambridge.org/

http://en.wikipedia.org/wiki/

http://encarta.msn.com/encnet/features/dictionary/

http://www.merriam-webster.com/

http://www.onelook.com/

http://jobs.blogs.ozfreeonline.com/2007/02/23/career-opportunity-for-chefs/

Chapter 6 Culinary Verbs

These are over 130 culinary verbs used to describe the process of cooking in the kitchen. The meanings and example sentences of culinary verbs are introduced. You have to commit to memory by repeatedly reading the meanings and example sentences of culinary verbs.

A

-add : to put something with something else to increase the number or amount or to improve the whole

ex) Beat the butter and sugar together and slowly add the eggs.

-adjust : to change something slightly, especially to make it more correct, effective, or suitable

ex) Adjust seasonings to taste.

-arrange : to put something in a particular order

ex) Arrange ham slices over cheese.

B

-bake : to cook inside a cooker, without using added liquid or fat

ex) Bake for 5~7 minutes in a preheated oven.

–baste : to pour hot fat and liquid over meat while it is cooking

ex) Baste the turkey at regular intervals.

–beat : to stir a mixture rapidly with a spoon or beater to make it light, fluffy, and smooth

ex) Beat the egg yolk very well in a mixing bowl.

–blacken : to become or make black or dark

ex) Grill the peppers whole, turning at intervals, until the skin is blackened.

–blanch : to put vegetables or similar foods into boiling water for a few minutes to make them white, remove the skins, get rid of strong flavours, or prepare them for freezing

ex) The most convenient way to blanch vegetables is in a large kettle of boiling water.

–blend : to mix two or more ingredients until they are smooth

ex) Blend the ingredients into a smooth paste.

–boil :

① to reach, or cause something to reach, the temperature at which a liquid starts to turn into a gas

ex) If you give water to a small baby to drink, you have to boil it first.

② to heat a container, especially one used for cooking, until the liquid in it starts to turn into a gas

ex) Could you boil the kettle for me?

③ to cook food by putting it in water that is boiling

ex) I've boiled some potatoes for dinner.

–braise : to cook food slowly in a covered dish in a little fat and liquid

ex) Braise greens by heating a little olive oil over medium heat.

–break : to split into smaller units, parts

ex) Break the biscuits into small pieces directly into a large bowl.

–broil (US FOR grill) : to cook something by direct heat, especially under a very hot surface in a cooker

ex) Broil for 5 to 7 minutes until skin is crisp and fish is cooked through.

–brown : to make food brown by cooking it:

ex) Lightly brown the onion before adding the tomatoes.

C

–caramelize : to cook a food with sugar so that the food becomes sweet and often brown

ex) Another way of making this dressing is to caramelize the shallots in a sauté pan instead of roasting them.

–carve sth up : to divide something into smaller parts

ex) Be sure you know how to carve up the apple.

–char : to burn and become black or to burn something so that it becomes black

ex) For easy peeling, grill the peppers until the skin starts to char.

–chill : to (cause to) become cold but not freeze

ex) Chill until ready to eat.

–chop : to cut something into pieces with an axe, knife or other sharp instrument

ex) Chop (up) the onions and carrots roughly.

–combine : to be joined or mixed together, or join or mix people or things together

ex) Combine all ingredients in a sauce pan and mix well.

–concasser : to chop roughly

ex) It is often used in connection with tomatoes, as in "Breaded Cutlet of Veal with Concassser Tomatoes."

–coat : to cover something with a layer of a particular substance

ex) Coat the fruit using the basting brush with the egg whites.

–cook : to make food safe and appetizing by heating it, or undergo heating in order to become ready to eat

ex) Cook the beef until it is tender.

–cream : to make food into a smooth thick liquid:

ex) Cream the butter and sugar together.

–crumble : to break, or cause something to break, into small pieces

ex) When they are crispy, crumble them with your hands and sprinkle them on the pizza.

-crush : to reduce fruit or vegetables to juice and pulp by pressing

ex Crush the garlic clove.

-cube : to cut food into cubes

ex) Cube the bread and cut the apples into chunks.

-cut : to divide food materials with a knife or scissors

ex) Cut the meat up into small pieces

D

-dampen(ALSO damp) : to make something slightly wet

ex) Dampen a cloth or paper towel with water.

-debone : to remove the bones from meat or fish

ex) There are many ways to debone a chicken.

-deep-fry : to fry food in a deep pan in which the food is completely covered by oil

ex) Cut them into slices and coat them in batter and deep-fry them.

-deglaze : dilute meat sediments in (a pan) to make a gravy or sauce

ex) Deglaze frying pan with 1/2 cup water.

-dice : to cut an ingredient into a small square shape

ex) Peel and dice the potatoes.

-dilute : to make a liquid weaker by mixing in something else ex) Dilute the juice (with water) before you drink it.

-dip : to put something briefly into a liquid

ex) Dip the fish in the batter, then drop it into the hot oil.

-dissolve : to be absorbed by a liquid, especially when mixed, or (of a liquid) to absorb a solid

ex) Dissolve the agar in liquid.

-divide : to (cause to) separate into parts or groups

ex) Divide it into 2 equal pieces.

-douse : to make something or someone wet by throwing a lot of liquid over them

ex) Don't forget to serve cold water to douse the flames.

-drain : to cause (a liquid) to flow away or cause a liquid to flow away from (something), leaving it dryer, or to become dryer as a liquid flows away

ex) Drain the pasta thoroughly. Drain (off) any liquid that is left in the rice.

-dredge : to cover before cooking

ex) Put flour in a shallow baking dish which is large enough to allow you to dredge fish fillets.

-dress : to add a liquid, especially a mixture of oil and vinegar, to a salad for additional flavour

ex) Dress some watercress with olive oil and lemon juice.

-drizzle : to pour very small quantities of a liquid in a thin stream over food

ex) Lightly drizzle the dressing over the vegetables.

-dust : to cover something with a light powder

ex) Lightly dust the work surface with flour.

F

-fill : to make or become full; to use empty space:

ex) Fill a deep fryer with corn oil, no more than 1/3 full.

-flambé : to pour liquor over food and light it in order to burn off the alcohol and impart the flavor of the liquor to the food

ex) Heat the foods you want to flambé in a deep, round, long-handled pan.

-flatten : to make something flat or flatter, or become flat or flatter

ex) Flatten chicken to 1/4-inch thickness, using a meat mallet.

-flip : to cause (something) to turn over quickly one or more times, or to cause (something) to move by making a short, quick motion

ex) With a little practice, any cook can learn to flip food in a pan.

-fold *sth* in/fold *sth* into something : to mix a substance into another substance by turning it gently with a spoon

ex) Fold the egg whites into the cake mixture.

-form : make or be made into a certain form.

ex) Form the sausage into patties and cook in a skillet over medium heat until brown.

-freeze : to prcserve food by storing it at a very low temperature so that it becomes hard

ex) Freeze ripe bananas for later use.

-frost : to cover a cake with frosting

ex) Leave the cake to cool before frosting it.

G

-gel : to change from a liquid into a thick soft solid

ex) Agar, also know as agar agar, is a nearly tasteless sea vegetable that is used for gelling liquids.

-glaze : to spread a layer of fat, jelly, jam, syrup or oil over a finished dish as a means of garnish or preserving

ex) Then continue to glaze the cake until the glaze is all used up.

-grate : to rub food against a grater in order to cut it into a lot of small pieces

ex) This recipe is easy if you have a food processor to grate your carrots.

-griddle : to cook something on a flat hot surface

ex) Griddle or toast the slices of bread

–grill : to cook something by direct heat, especially under a very hot surface in a cooker

ex) Grill the chicken wings directly over a medium heat.

H

–halve : to reduce something by half or divide something into two equal pieces

ex) Halve hard–cooked eggs lengthwise.

I

–immerse : to put something or someone completely under the surface of a liquid

ex) The shells should be immersed in boiling water for two minutes.

–incorporate : to include something as part of something larger

ex) Sauté these ingredients until they are incorporated into a sauce.

J

–julienne : to finely slice an ingredient into 'needle-like shreds'. A julienne, although thinner than a 'baton' should be of the same length

ex) Julienne the ginger piece and keep aside.

K

-knead : to press something, especially a mixture for making bread, firmly and repeatedly with the hands and fingers

ex) Knead the dough until smooth and elastic.

L

-ladle : to put soup or other liquid food into bowls to give to people, using a ladle

ex) Ladle into small demitasse cups and serve.

-layer : to arrange something in layers

ex) Layer the pasta with slices of tomato.

-line : to cover the inner surface of something

ex) Line a tray with greaseproof paper and rub it with olive oil.

M

-macerate : to soak food in a liquid as a means of marinating or infusing flavours. (Traditionally done to fresh and dried fruits)

ex) Mix together all the ingredients and leave them to macerate in the fridge overnight.

-marinate : to be placed or soaked in a marinade, or place or soak food in a marinade

ex) Marinate the chicken in white wine for a couple of hours before frying.

-mash : to crush food, usually after cooking it, so that it forms a soft mass

ex) Mash the potatoes and then mix in the butter and herbs.

-melt : to turn from something solid into something soft or liquid, or to cause something to do this

ex) Melt 2 tablespoons of butter in a saucepan over medium-high heat.

-microwave : to heat or cook food or beverages in a microwave

ex) Microwave a lemon for 15 seconds and double the juice you get before squeezing.

-mince : to cut meat, or other food, into very small pieces, sometimes using a special machine

ex) Mince two pounds of chicken finely.

P

-parboil : to partially cook or soften an ingredient by boiling

ex) Parboil small, waxy potatoes until tender before grilling.

-pare : to remove the skin or outer layer of something such as a vegetable or fruit thinly and neatly

ex) Prepare watermelon rinds by paring off the dark green outer cover and removing the pink meat.

-pat : to touch someone or something gently and usually repeatedly with the hand flat

ex) Pat the balls lightly with shortening and let rest for 20 minutes.

-peel : to remove the skin of fruit and vegetables

ex) Peel the skin from the cucumber using a vegetable peeler.

-poach : to cook something such as a fish, or an egg with its shell removed, by putting it in gently boiling water or other liquid

ex) We had poached eggs for breakfast. Do you like pears poached in red wine?

-pound : to hit or beat repeatedly with a lot of force, or to crush something by hitting it repeatedly

ex) Pound the meat with your hand or a kitchen tool.

-pour : to make a substance flow from a container, especially into another container, by raising just one side of the container that the substance is in

ex) Pour the honey into the bowl and mix it thoroughly with the other ingredients.

-preheat : to heat a cooker to a particular temperature before putting food in it

ex) Preheat oven to 365 degrees F.

-pry : to move or lift something by pressing a tool against a fixed point

ex) Using small heavy knife, pry large pieces of soft coconut meat out of shells.

-purée : to make fruit or vegetables into a thick smooth sauce by crushing them, usually in a machine

ex) Puree yams in blender to about the same consistency as the pumpkin.

-put : to move something or someone into the stated place, position or direction ex) He put salt into the sugar bowl by mistake.

R

-reduce: to reduce an amount of liquid through boiling to thicken a sauce, liquid or syrup

ex) To make a thicker sauce, reduce the ingredients by boiling for 5 minutes. Reduce the oven temperature to 325 degrees F.

-refresh : to run an ingredient beneath cold (or sometimes hot) water to prevent further cooking, prevent colour loss and to remove excess starch

ex) Refresh vegetables under cold running water and set aside.

-remove : to take something or someone away from somewhere, or off something

ex) Do you know how to remove the seeds from raspberry jam? Remove top of boiler from heat.

-rinse : to use water to clean the soap or dirt from something

ex) Rinse chicken with cold water and pat dry with paper towels.

-rip : to roughly tear something apart or off, or become torn in this way

ex) It's important to try to push your hand gently down the breast, being careful not to rip the skin.

-roast : to cook food in an oven or over a fire

ex) Just roast the chicken in the oven and baste it in oil and lemon.

-roll : to (cause something to) turn over onto itself to form a cylinder or a sphere ex) He rolled the dough into small balls in his hands.

-rub : move over something with pressure

ex) Rub garlic herb mixture over lamb.

-sauté : to cook food in oil or fat over heat, usually until it is brown

ex) Sauté peppers and ham in olive oil for 3 minutes and season with pepper.

S

-scald : to heat at a simmer or the point just before boiling

ex) Scald the milk and then add it to the egg and sugar mixture.

-scoop : to move something with a scoop or with something used as a scoop

ex) Scoop all seeds out.

-scramble : to beat eggs, usually with some milk, and cook while stirring in a pan until set

ex) Scramble the eggs in a shallow, wide bowl.

-scrape : to remove an unwanted covering or a top layer from something, especially using a sharp edge or something rough

ex) Scrape bottom with a wooden spoon.

-scrub : to rub something hard in order to clean it, especially using a stiff brush, soap and water

ex) He scrubbed the old saucepan clean, and it looked as good as new.

–seal : to cover a surface with a special liquid to protect it

ex) Seal the edges with water.

–sear : to fry a piece of meat quickly at a high temperature, in order to prevent liquid and flavour escaping from it

ex) Searing meat on the stove caramelizes its sugars and amplifies flavor.

–season : to improve the flavour of savoury food by adding salt, herbs or spices when cooking or preparing it

ex) Season the meat with salt, pepper and herbs, if desired.

–serve : to provide food or drinks

ex) Serve the fish and vegetables with the warm sauce poured over the top.

–separate : to (cause to) divide into parts

ex) Separate the egg yolks from the whites.

–sever : to break or separate, especially by cutting

ex) Cut through the joint to sever the leg.

–shake : to move backwards and forwards or up and down in quick, short movements, or to make something or someone do this

ex) Shake the pan back and forth until all of the flames have died out.

–shallow–fry : to cook food in a small amount of oil or fat

ex) Shallow–fry the fish/bacon.

-shred : to cut or tear something roughly into thin strips

ex) Shred the lettuce and arrange it around the edge of the dish.

-sieve : to put a liquid or powder through a sieve

ex) Sieve the flour and baking powder into the butter mixture.

-sift : to put dry ingredients such as flour or sugar through a screen or sifter

ex) When the cake is cooked, sift some icing sugar over the top of it.

-simmer : to cook something liquid, or something with liquid in it, at a temperature slightly below boiling

ex) Simmer over low heat for at least two hours.

-skim : to remove something solid from the surface of a liquid

ex) Skim fat from the broth.

-slice : to cut something into thin, flat pieces

ex) Slice the mushrooms thinly and fry in butter.

-slit : to make a long straight narrow cut in something

ex) Slit the potatoes lengthwise about two inches.

-smash : to break something into many small pieces, or be broken in this way

ex) Using a mortar and pestle, smash a few cloves of garlic.

-smear : to spread a liquid or a thick substance over a surface ex) Smear butter around the inside of a baking dish.

–smoke : to preserve meat, fish or cheese using smoke from burning wood

ex) She had champagne and smoked salmon sandwiches at her birthday party.

–soak : to make very wet, or (of liquid) to be absorbed in large amounts

ex) Soak the meat in clean, fresh water for 24 hours in the refrigerator.

–spice : to use spice to add flavour to food or drink

ex) Spicing it up with exotic herbs.

–spoon : to move something, especially food, using a spoon

ex) Spoon shrimp with sauce over pasta, and top with Parmesan cheese.

–spread : to (cause to) cover, reach or have an effect on a wider or increasing area

ex) Spread 1 tablespoon mustard on each Boboli(baked cheese pizza crusts).

–sprinkle : to scatter a few bits or drops of something over a surface

ex) Sprinkle a few herbs on the pizza. Sprinkle the pizza with a few herbs.

–squeeze : to press something firmly, especially from all sides in order to change its shape, reduce its size or remove liquid from it

ex) Cut the lemon in half and squeeze the juice into the bowl.

-steam : to cook food using steam

ex) Steam the carrot and bell pepper until they are a bright color, but still crunchy.

-stew : to cook meat, fish, vegetables or fruit slowly and gently in a little liquid

ex) Stew lamb pieces with chopped potatoes and sliced onion.

-stir : to mix a liquid or other substance by moving an object such as a spoon in a circular pattern

ex) Stir the sauce gently until it begins to boil. Stir the egg yolks into the mixture.

-strain : to separate liquid food from solid food, especially by pouring it through a utensil with small holes in it

ex) Strain the custard through a fine sieve into a clean container.

-stuff : to fill something with stuffing

ex) Stuff this filling into your bell peppers (cherry peppers) and serve on a plate as tapas.

-sweat : to gently cook

ex) Here's how to sweat onions in a few steps.

T

-tear : to pull or be pulled apart, or to pull pieces off

ex) Tear the broccoli and cauliflower into small florets.

–thaw : to (cause to) change from a solid, frozen state to a liquid or soft one, because of an increase in temperature

ex) The best way to thaw shrimp is to put them in a bowl of warm water.

–thicken : to become thick or thicker, or make something thick or thicker

ex) Use a cornstarch slurry to thicken fruit and vegetable juices.

–thread : to put something long and thin such as string or thread through a narrow hole or into a small space

ex) Thread chicken onto skewers.

–tilt : to (cause to) move into a sloping position

ex) Tilt the pan away from you.

–tip : to pour a substance from one container into another or onto a surface

ex) Don't tip or spill pan contents.

–top : to put a topping on something (often passive)

ex) Top with remaining cheese and dust with paprika.

–toast : to make bread or other food warm, crisp and brown by putting it near a high heat

ex) Do you want this bread toasted?

–toss : to mix something, especially a salad with its dressing, by lifting and turning its parts rather than by stirring ex) Tossing pizza dough isn't just a way to show off your culinary skills. Toss all of the sliced ingredients into a large bowl with the mixed greens, walnuts and cheese.

-transfer : to move someone or something from one place, vehicle, person or group to another

ex) Transfer the marinade and lamb to a plastic bag and seal.

-trim : to make something tidier or more level by cutting a small amount off it

ex) Trim off the ends.

-turn : to move, or to move an object or page, so that a different side or surface is on the top

ex) Place egg rolls into heated oil and fry, turning occasionally, until golden brown. Turn the heat up to medium-high.

W

-whip : to beat food, especially cream with a special utensil in order to make it thick and firm

ex) Could you whip the cream for me?

-whisk : to beat eggs, cream, etc. with a special utensil in order to add air and make the food light

ex) Whisk the egg whites until stiff.

Z

-zest : to grate the outer layer of a citrus fruit

ex) She knows how to zest a lemon, lime or orange.

N.o.t.e

-icing : a mixture of sugar with liquid or fat, used as a coating or filling for cakes or biscuits

-fluffy : (of food) light in texture

-greens : the leaves of green vegetables such as spinach or cabbage when eaten as food

-chunk : a roughly cut lump

-impart : to give something a particular feeling, quality or taste

-elastic : describes material that is able to stretch and be returned to its original shape or size

-demitasse : a small cup of coffee, or the cup in which such coffee is served

-rind : the hard outer layer or covering of particular fruits and foods

-consistency : the physical nature of a substance, especially a thick liquid, for example by being thick or thin, smooth or lumpy

-sphere : an object shaped like a round ball

-amplify : to increase the size or effect of something

-died out : to become less common and finally stop existing

-mesh : (a piece of) net-like material with spaces in it, made from wire, plastic or thread

-floret : a small flower-like part of a vegetable

-slurry : a mixture of water and small pieces of a solid, especially such a mixture used in an industrial or farming process
-show off : to behave in a way which is intended to attract attention or admiration, and which other people often find annoying

-stiff : firm or hard

R.e.f.e.r.n.c.e.s

http://dictionary.cambridge.org/

http://en.wikipedia.org/wiki/

http://encarta.msn.com/encnet/features/dictionary/

http://www.french-at-a-touch.com/Words-Phrases/kitchen_words_phrases_a_-_n.htm

http://www.merriam-webster.com/

http://www.onelook.com/

http://agexted.cas.psu.edu/FCS/4hfl/PortableKitchen.html

http://esl.about.com/library/vocabulary/blwordgroups_food.htm

http://www.cooking4chumps.com/Lingo%20Kitchen%20Vocabulary%20Language.html

http://www.englishclub.com/english-for-work/food-drink-back.htm

http://www.ehow.com/

Chinese Cuisine Training Institute, Art of Beijing and Shandong Cuisines (Food Paradise Publishing Co., Quarry Bay Hongkong, 2007

Guide to Kitchen Enlgish

Part Ⅱ

Expressions
Coversations
Idioms
Quizzes & Puzzles

" Find the best and freshest ingredients you possibly can_ then prepare them simply. " _Tim Creehan

Chapter 7 Expressions used in The Kitchen

Working in the food and beverage industry may also mean working where the food gets stored, prepared, and cooked. The kitchen area, which is also where the dishes get cleaned, is commonly referred to as the back of the house. Whether the establishment is a restaurant, cafe, or fast-food joint, there are a number of different jobs in the back of the house, all requiring different types of English skills. Even though you may not have to deal with English guests directly, you will have to understand their needs. You may also need to communicate with coworkers whose first language is English.

1. Wait staff to Chef

Below are common expressions used in the kitchen between wait staff and chef. Let's look at them.

- Can you put a rush on table two' s order?
- What's the ETA (estimated time of arrival) on the lasagna?
- How much longer for the roasted chicken?
- What's the soup of the day?
- One of my customers wants to know what you put in your cream sauce.
- Didn't I punch in a garlic bread with cheese?
- I'm missing three side salads.
- Table seven said to give compliments to the chef.

- My customer says this hamburger isn't cooked enough.
- Are you too busy to make me a staff meal?
- How much should I charge for an extra side of salsa?
- Oh, they're not going to be happy about that.

2. Chef to Wait staff

Below are common expressions used in the kitchen between chef and wait staff. Let's look at them.

- Can you run this food? It's getting cold.
- The special is a rack of lamb with a tossed salad.
- I can do it, but it's going to cost extra.
- We just got five orders at once.
- It's going to be another minute for the rice.
- Are all of these separate cheques for the same table?
- Did you want the chicken wings to come up first?
- You asked for that hot sauce on the side, right?
- How does your table like their cheesecake?
- Don't forget to punch in those salads.
- Taste this soup and tell me what you think.
- Tell them ice cream for dessert is on me.
- Tell them we can do roasted or mashed potatoes instead.
- It's to go with the kids' meals.
- Ask her what they want instead.
- Can you tell Anna there's no fries left for her table's order?

3. Among Kitchen Staff members

Below are common expressions used in the kitchen between chef to kitchen staff and vice versa. Let's look at them.

- Should I get the salads and soups ready?
- We need five caesar salads and two soups of the day.
- Should I get the steaks on the grill?
- I thought we were all out of fries?
- Have you ever made some desert?
- Can you cook well? What?
- How often do you cook?
- How do you cook shabu shabu?
- What kind of nabe cooking do you like?
- What do you put on a fried egg? scrambled eggs? french toast?
- Please close the refrigerator.
- Don't hold the refrigerator door open.
- Jane, it's your turn to do the dishes.
- I'll wash the dishes and you can dry.
- Is supper ready yet?
- When will dinner be ready?
- Tom, will you please load the dishwasher?
- Put the dirty dishes in the sink.
- We need an extra chair.
- The turkey is in the oven.
- I'll warm up the pizza in the microwave.
- Don't put those bones in the garbage disposal.
- Please put the silverware on the table.

- Use one squirt of dish detergent when you wash dishes.
- The broom and mop are standing in the closet.
- The dustpan is in there, too, hanging on a hook.
- I need the mixer to blend the cake ingredients.
- I have to put the groceries away.
- Put the plates and saucers in the cupboard.
- Put the cups and glasses in the other cupboard.
- I have to scour the large pan.
- Put some bread in the toaster.
- Where should I put the canned goods?
- Cleaning products belong in the cupboard under the sink.
- Boxes of cereal and crackers go in the cupboard over the sink.
- Please put a new roll of paper towels in the dispenser.
- I have to sweep and mop the kitchen floor.
- Please get a bucket of soapy water for me.
- Rinse the dishes before you put them in the dish washer.
- Will you put the silverware in the drawer?
- Do you know what tsp stands for? Show in your hand how much 1tsp is.
- How many ml (millilitres) are there in $\frac{3}{4}$ cup?
- How would you know how much milk to use in this recipe?
- What shape is a head of cabbage? Can you use any kind of cabbage for this recipe?
- What do you think baste means?
- We need to prepare a half-pan of tomatoes and a batch of sauce.
- we need to prepare a tray of beef and cut forty chickens.
- We need to prepare a tub of spaghetti and a pan of parsley.
- Take the dirty knife to the dish machine.
- Walk with the blade down.
- Put the knife in the dish rack.

- Walk with the blade down and give it to the manager.
- Pick up the knife.
- Look at it.
- Check it out.
- Put the mushroom on the cutting board.
- Oops! The cutting board is moving. Put a mat under the cutting board
- Good Work!
- Don't chop the mushroom.
- Cut away from your body.
- Check the blade and the tray.
- Slice the eggplant.
- Be careful! Don't touch the blade.
- Unplug the slicer.
- Say "hot stuff" next time.
- Bring me some lettuce.
- Bring me more soup.
- Open the sanitizer.
- Bring me the sanitizer bucket.
- Put it back in the bucket.
- Keep it clean.
- Take the sauce to the cook.
- Get some shrimp from the freezer.
- Pour floor cleanser and water into the bucket.
- Mop the floor toward the drain.
- Use the squeegee to push the water to the drain.
- Don't pick up the broken glass with your hands!
- Show the manager the cut.
- Put antiseptic on your wound.
- Wrap it in a clean bandage.

- Don't touch the handle on that hot pan!
- Show him/her your wound.
- Put your hand in cold water.
- Cover the burn with a clean, dry pad.

N.o.t.e

–**joint** : INFORMAL, a bar or restaurant which serves cheap food and drink

–**rush** : when you have to hurry or move somewhere quickly

–**punch in** : to enter information into a computer using the keyboard

–**compliment** : a remark or action that expresses approval, admiration, or respect

–**run** : to carry out or accomplish something

–**rack** : a large piece of meat cut from the neck of a sheep

–**on the side** : MAINLY US (of food in a restaurant) served on another plate, or not on part of the meal

–**load** : to put into a machine the items that it will work on, e.g. clothes for washing

–**warm *sth* up** : to heat food that has already been cooked

–**squirt** : an amount of liquid or gas that is squirted out

–**dustpan** : a flat container with a handle into which you brush dust and dirt

–**scour** : to remove dirt from something by rubbing it hard with something rough

–**squeegee** : a tool with a rubber blade and a short handle which is used for removing water from a surface such as a window or mirror after it has been washed

–**antiseptic** : a chemical used for preventing infection in an injury, especially by killing bacteria

R.e.f.e.r.n.c.e.s

http://www.englishclub.com/english-for-work/food-drink-back.htm

http://dictionary.cambridge.org/

http://en.wikipedia.org/wiki/

http://encarta.msn.com/encnet/features/dictionary/

http://www.merriam-webster.com/

http://www.onelook.com/

Chapter 8 Conversations about Food and Cooking

1. A Chef's Life

Rebecca talks about her experience working in restaurants.

Todd: So, Rebecca, now you were saying that you were a chef, or you worked in a kitchen in your previous job. Can you talk about that? Like where did you work and what was it like?

Rebecca: OK, I worked in a few different restaurants over several years, sometimes full-time, sometimes part-time. Sometimes I worked in busy city restaurants, and other times just small cafes doing breakfast, that kind of thing.

Todd: OK, so, you must have had a very busy routine. Can you describe what's the typical workday when you are a chef?

Rebecca: Well, usually you start preparing in the afternoon and that's the quiet part of the day. You don't have any customers. You just come in and you chop up all the vegetables and the things you need to do like that. You cook any food that can be cooked before and organize all the ingredients for the dishes. Then service starts at about six o'clock and that's when it gets really crazy. It's really busy from then on and you have to be very organized and cook everything as fast as possible.

Todd : OK, sounds like a pretty busy schedule. When you're working, what do you enjoy about the job? What makes the job fun and interesting?

Rebecca : Actually, I like the pressure of cooking. It's stressful but it's also exciting. It's like a game. You have to organize everything, and you have to think of sixty things at once. It's a really good atmosphere. Everybody's excited. Everyone has to work together. It's a team job, so you can make really close friends in the kitchen. It's fun to work with them.

Todd : Is there anything you didn't like? Like maybe the smell of the food or getting dirty or things like that?

Rebecca : No, that didn't bother me, but I used to travel home after work on the bus sometimes and interestingly even when it was full I would have a seat to myself because the smell of the food gets into your clothes, your hair, your skin, everything. You smell like fifty different kinds of food. That's not a good thing.

Todd : Wow. So did you have dogs or anything when you got home that they would be like craving for you to walk through the door?

Rebecc a: No, I didn't have dogs because I was scared they might eat me you know. They might think I was a piece of steak or something.

Todd : Alright thanks, Rebecca.

2. How to be a Chef

Rebecca discusses the various ways one can become a chef.

Todd : OK, Rebecca we're talking about working in a restaurant. Now you became a chef. Can you talk about the process of becoming a chef? What do you do to get a job in a kitchen?

Rebecca : Well, there's lots of different ways, but the most common way is to become an apprentice which means you go to the kitchen and work at the bottom level doing the basic chopping—boring jobs—for maybe two or three years, and then one day a week you go to school, a cooking school. Your employer pays for you to go to the school. You do get paid by your employer but it's a really small wage, so, yeah. Otherwise, you can start at the bottom, like a dishwasher, and actually Australia's most famous chef started that way. He just was a dishwasher and he slowly climbed up the ladder, so you can do it that way as well.

Todd : So what about you? Did you go to cooking school?

Rebecca : Yeah, I did, but actually I dropped out after a while, so I did that for about a year but to be honest I think you get more experience in a kitchen. Sometimes the stuff they teach you at school is a little bit old-fashioned.

Todd : How much actually of what you learn do you just learn on yourself, as just a creative process? Like how much do you think you learn by watching others and how much do you learn on your own, using your own creativity?

Rebecca : I think both are really important. Actually, I learned a lot from my mother. When I was a kid, I used to watch her cooking all the time, and it wasn't until I grew up that I realized how much I understood about cooking just from seeing what she did in the kitchen, but also talking about how to do things with your colleagues I think is really important.

Todd : Now, I'm curious, you know how to cook, and everybody knows you know how to cook-family members and friends-so how... do you like to actually cook for family members and friends or is cooking a job that when you go home, you prefer not to cook for other people because it's like bringing your work home?

Rebecca : Well, I know some chefs that have nothing in their fridge and they hate cooking at home, but I'm not like that. I really love cooking for people. It's really the nicest thing you can do for someone is to give them a lovely meal. The sad thing is actually that no one will ever cook for me, because they're too scared. They always apologize before I even have a chance to eat it. "Oh, it's going to be terrible. Oh, you're a cook. I'm sorry." But actually I love food being cooked for me. I wish people would do it more.

Todd : OK. That's funny. Thanks Rebecca.

3. Kitchen Safety

Rebecca talks about the dangers of working in a restaurant and kitchen safety.

Todd : Now, Rebecca, we're talking about working in the kitchen. I was a waiter and when I would help out in the kitchen, I was always afraid of the big knives and the fires and the burns and stuff, so can you talk a little about safety and maybe about some injuries you had working in the kitchen?

Rebecca : Yeah, that's really important actually. First there's the uniform. You have to cover as much of your skin as you can to avoid burns and if you have a special chef jacket, it must be all cotton so if you get something hot on it, it will still be safe, and it can be quickly taken off, so if you spill something very hot on your clothes, you actually remove the top layer and then you have something underneath, so you can avoid the hot thing being on your skin.

Todd : Well, have you ever been burned, and when you are burned what do you do to your skin to make the burn go away?

Rebecca : Yeah, I've only ever had one bad burn. It was from pork fat and I burnt my arm. I had a horrible blister afterwards, but you have to be careful not to touch the burn or break it. You should of course immediately put in under cold water and then afterwards I use vitamin E oil and that was really good, actually. I don't have a scar because I used that and the skin healed really well.

Todd : What about cuts? I imagine you must have a million cuts from all those big sharp knives. What do you do for that?

Rebecca : Actually, I've never, never cut myself. Never, never. No!

Because they teach you when you learn how to chop a way to keep all your fingers out away from the knife and you always have the knife in contact with your hand so you don't need to look at it when you cut. You can feel where the knife is. And no, I've never cut myself.

Todd : That's pretty impressive. Wow! OK, Now, last thing. I guess the only danger I would see in the kitchen is just slipping and falling. The floor is always wet and greasy or whatever. What do you do about that?

Rebecca : You wear really, really heavy boots. I had a huge pair of boots, and of course we clean the floors really carefully. At the end of every shift, you get rid of as much grease as possible and we use non-slip mats, so that helps.

Todd : Cool. Thanks for the safety tips, Rebecca. Thanks.

4. Recipe

Alexandra gives her special Cuban recipe.

Todd : Alexandra, you were saying that you can cook Cuban food.

Alexandra: Yes, yes. It's very good stuff, and I've got one recipe that comes to mind that has to do with chicken and rice. You can take several pieces of chicken and boil them in water with some salt until the chicken is cooked. You take out the pieces and with a couple of forks, shred the meat. In a pan you put garlic, onions, olive oil, and tomatoes. Fry that up. Put the chicken on top and then put a puree of tomatoes on top of that and just saute that for a while and you can put it over white rice and you'll have yourself a nice meal

Todd : Wow, that sounds pretty good.

Alexandra: Yeah, it's very good, and for a change you can always add green peppers, red peppers and make it very colorful, and serve it with some white plantains and a little Cuban drink and you are good to go.

Todd : Alright, thanks. I'm gonna give that a try.

Quizzes about Recipe

1) What do you do first?

a) Boil the chicken b) Fry the chicken c) Shred the meat

2) What do you put in the boiling water?

a) Chicken b) Salt c) Both

3) What do you use to shred the meat?

a) Shredder b) Your hands c) Forks

4) What can make it colorful?

a) Peppers b) Berries c) Mint leaves

5) What can you serve it with?

a) Plantains b) Cuban drink c) Both

5. Tacos

Anna talks about how she like to make tacos.

Todd : OK, now Anna, you were saying that your favorite food is tacos.

Anna : Yes, it is.

Todd : OK, and how do you make tacos?

Anna : They're pretty easy. All you do is, buy some meat like ground beef, or ground turkey, and you cook it in a skillet until it's finished. You can add some chopped onion, or any spices, like cumin or chili powder and then you just serve the meat on tortillas or taco shell with cheese, tomato, lettuce, onion, guacamole, or anything. They're delicious.

Todd : Sounds pretty good. So what do you put the meat in? The meat has to go on a tortilla or something?

Anna : Yeah, on the tortilla.

Todd : Oh, OK.

Anna : And you can add on top.

Todd : OK, what kind of tortillas do you use, flour or corn?

Anna : I like corn but my husband John, he likes flour. We make both.

Quizzes about Tacos

1) What kinds of meat does she like to use?

a) Beef b) Turkey c) Both

2) What do you use to cook the meat?

a) Grill b) Skillet c) Pot

3) What is something you can add to the tacos?

a) Spices b) Dressing c) Sauce

4) Where do you put the meat ?

a) In a tortilla　　b) In bread　　c) On chips

5) What kind of tortilla does John like?

a) Flour　　b) Corn　　c) Wheat

6. Veggies
Ruth and Todd talk about the vegetables.

Todd : So, Ruth, now, you are a vegetarian.

Ruth : That's right.

Todd : So what is a good vegetarian dish that you cook?

Ruth : Well, actually, I'm not a very good cook, so that would be difficult to say. I quite like to make, like a vegetable stew with tofu in it. Things like that, but it's not very exciting.

Todd : Well, how do you make the stew?

Ruth : Well, firstly, you get all of the vegetable ready and so you chop them up and the potatoes and you boil the potatoes and then you boil the other vegetables, and you fry the tofu with onions and then I think you just put it all together in a pan and stick it in the oven, I think.

Todd : Sounds pretty good.

Ruth : It's very easy.

Todd : What vegetables do you usually put inside the stew?

Ruth : Oh, things like carrots and leaks and courgettes sometimes, mushrooms, and really any vegetables that are in season that I can get hold of.

Todd : Courgettes? Is that squash? Zucchini?

Ruth : I think it might be squash. No, I think it's zucchini.

Todd : Zucchini.

Ruth : I think it's zucchini.

Todd : OK, yeah, I think in the states we call it zucchini.

Ruth : And you would call aubergine, eggplant.

Todd : Yes. What do you call eggplant?

Ruth : Aubergine.

Todd : Aubergine.

Ruth : Yeah.

Todd : How do you spell it?

Ruth : Good question. A-U-B-E-R-G-I-N-E.

Todd : Wow. How do you spell courgettes?

Ruth : C-O-U-R-G-E-T-T-E

Todd : That's pretty good. Now can you spell Zucchini?

Ruth : Probably not. Z-U-C-C-H-I-N-I.

Todd : Yeah, maybe that's it. One more time.

Ruth : Z-U-C-C-H-I-N-I.

Todd : Yeah, I think that's it. Zucchini. I'm not even sure.

Ruth : I'm not either.

Todd : Yeah, what's your favorite vegetable?

Ruth : Ah, it has to be broccoli.

Todd : Oh, yeah?

Ruth : I really like broccoli. They look like little trees, there that's nice.

Todd : Yeah, that's true. Yeah, if you just get one broccoli and start eating it, you can't even finish it. It's just so big.

Ruth : Oh, you can. You definitely can.

Todd : Well, how do you cook your broccoli?

Ruth : Just very briefly really because there's nothing worse than soggy broccoli. You cook it. You boil it in a pan with water only for a three or four minutes. What's your favorite vegetable?

Todd : That's a good question. I would have to go with the eggplant and the "aubergine"?

Ruth : Aubergine.

Todd : Aubergine. So the aubergine as you call it, yeah.

Ruth : I think eggplant's the best. Really, don't you think they're sometimes a bit soggy?

Todd : Actually I kind of like them that way.

Ruth : Really.

Todd : Yeah. I like them any way. Although the bad thing about the eggplant is you can't eat it raw.

Ruth : Yeah, that's true. It takes effort.

7. Cooking Tips
Akane gives cooking advice.

Todd : Hey, Akane, I know that you cook a lot, and I never cook, but it's starting to get really expensive to eat out so I wanna cook more.

Akane : Right.

Todd : Can you recommend something that is very, very easy for somebody who does not know how to cook.

Akane : OK, well, I'm not the best cook myself but I do cook often for financial reasons because it is cheaper. Um, I would recommend, if you're not used to cooking I would recommend the fried noodles. It's quick. It's easy. It's inexpensive, and yeah, I think you can do it.

Todd : Mm, OK, so what do I do? I mean actually, first of all, what do I need to buy?

Akane : Well, I think you would need to go to the grocery store and get some noodles. You can get the ready prepared ones which are quick and easy. The dried ones you would have to boil first, so I would prepare, I would recommend the ready prepared ones and you also need some vegetables, and maybe if you like you can also add some meats.

Todd : Mm, OK, I probably won't do the meat thing, but for the vegetables, what vegetables do you recommend?

Akane : Well, I recommend seasonal vegetables because the ones in season are always higher in vitamins and nutrients. Right now it's about early summer, late spring so the ones that are good right now egg plants, spinach and, well bean sprouts are good all year round.

Todd : Mm, OK, so assuming I buy all this stuff (right) bring it home, what do I do?

Akane : Well, first you need a good frying pan. (I got that) OK, first you actually need to wash the vegetables and cut them up into small pieces and then heat the pan up with oil and then put the vegetables in first because they take longer to cook than the noodles. After you have seen that the vegetables have gotten slightly brown and soft, then you can add the noodles and mix it up until the noodles are heated up and then just season it with salt and pepper or a sauce that you like.

Todd : OK, sounds pretty easy, but as for the oil, what kind of oil should I get?

Akane : Well, vegetable oil, canola oil, or olive oil, I think would be the healthiest choices.

Todd : OK, now one problem I have about cooking is, for people who don't know how to cook, how much do you cook? Like you said, chop up the vegetables (Yeah) Do I chop up five eggplants, one eggplant?

Akane : Well, if it's just for yourself, I would recommend just one eggplant and maybe half a bag of bean sprouts and half a bunch of spinach. The vegetables really shrink after you cook them so it might look like a lot when they're raw, but once you cook them. They shrink.

Todd : OK. Well, I'll give it a try, and I'll tell you how it tastes.

Akane : Great. Good luck.

8. How to Make Spaghetti
Akane shares her spaghetti recipe.

Hello, and welcome to our show.
Today, we'll be making one of my favourite recipes.
It's called the egg spaghetti.

First, what you will need for this recipe is:
About a hundred grams of dried spaghetti,
Two table spoons of olive oil,
Fifty grams of minced meat,
About a half of a medium onion,
Half a cup of chopped mushrooms,
One cup of tomato sauce, or peeled crushed tomatoes
(I prefer peeled crushed tomatoes)
And lastly, you will need one egg.

First, let your water come to a boil, and boil your dried spaghetti. While you are waiting for your spaghetti to boil, you can prepare your sauce.

Heat up the pan with the olive oil, and add the minced meat.
Brown the minced meat until it gets nice and brown.
Lower the heat to about medium heat, and then add your chopped onions.
It's important to fry your onions in lower heat so that you can let it caramelize.
It'll take a while but it will be worth the effort, because all of the sugars will come out of the onion and bring a nice sweet taste to your sauce.
Then, add your mushrooms (your chopped mushrooms), and keep stirring it around until it gets nice and tender.
And then lastly, you can add your tomato sauce, or peeled crushed tomatoes.
And let it simmer for a bit until it gets nice and warm.

Your spaghetti should be ready by now.

So you can drain the water out and add a bit of olive oil to your spaghetti, so that it won't stick.
Put your spaghetti on a plate, and then pour some of your sauce on top.

Now, you can fry your egg on a pan sunny-side-up.
I like to leave the yolk nice and soft.
And then put the fried egg on top of your spaghetti.
Now, when you eat your spaghetti, I like to pierce the egg with a fork so that all the yolk drizzles out and becomes a part of the sauce.
The egg is quite alkaline, so it brings a nice mild taste that counteracts with the acidic tomato.

And enjoy!

N.o.t.e

–routine : a habitual or fixed way of doing things

–get into : to become involved or absorbed in something

–crave : to beg or plead (usually fol. by for).

–apprentice : someone who has agreed to work for a skilled person for a particular period of time and often for low payment, in order to learn that person's skills

–slip : to slide unintentionally

–cool : excellent; very good

–plantain : a tropical fruit similar to a banana with green skin, or the plant that produces this fruit
-good to go : Ready for some specific task or ready for normal activity, especially after preparation or recovery

–cumin : (a plant with) seeds that smell pleasant and are used as a spice, especially in Indian and Middle Eastern cooking

–tortilla : a type of thin round Mexican bread made from maize flour and eggs

–guacamole : a thick mixture of avocado (= a savoury green tropical fruit), tomato, onion and spices, which is usually eaten cold

–stick : to push a pointed object into or through something, or (of a pointed object) to be pushed into or through something and stay there

–courgette(US zucchini) : a long thin vegetable with a dark green skin. It is a type of small marrow

–aubergine(US eggplant) : an oval purple vegetable which is white inside and which is usually eaten cooked

–soggy : (of things which can absorb water, especially food) unpleasantly wet and soft

–go with *sb/sth* (AGREE) : to accept an idea or agree with a person

–do : to cook or prepare food

N.o.t.e

-assuming (that) : accepting as true without question or proof

-canola oil : an edible vegetable oil obtained from the seeds of canola that is high in monounsaturated fatty acids

-counteract : to reduce or remove the effect of something unwanted by producing an opposite effect

R.e.f.e.r.n.c.e.s

http://www.elllo.org/english/0151/200-Anna-Tacos.htm

http://www.elllo.org/english/0151/161-Alexandra-Recipe.htm

http://www.elllo.org/english/0701/T724-Rebecca-Safety.htm

http://www.elllo.org/english/0701/T723-Rebecca-BecomingChef.htm

http://www.elllo.org/english/0451/452-Ruth-Vegetarian.htm

http://www.elllo.org/english/0451/474-Akane-Cooking.htm

http://www.elllo.org/english/0701/T722-Rebecca-ChefJob.htm

http://www.elllo.org/english/0451/481-Akane-Recipe.htm

http://dictionary.cambridge.org/

http://en.wikipedia.org/wiki/

http://encarta.msn.com/encnet/features/dictionary/

http://www.merriam-webster.com/

http://www.onelook.com/

Chapter 9 Food Idioms

This chapter introduces idioms of 15 kinds of food. All of these idioms have food in them. By showing how to use them in sentences these idioms help you understand of the metaphorical meanings of selected idioms in sentences. Let's get indulged in food idioms.

1. Apple Idioms

– **apple of (someone' s) eye** : someone or something that one likes a lot

ex) The little girl is the apple of her grandfather's eye.

– **as easy as apple pie** : very easy

ex) The test that I wrote yesterday was as easy as apple pie.

– **bad/rotten apple** : a bad person

ex) The boy is a bad apple and he is always in some kind of trouble.

– **compare apples and oranges** : to compare two things that are not similar and should not be compared

ex) It was like comparing apples and oranges when we compared our new boss to our old one.

- **polish the apple** : to flatter someone

  ex) Nobody likes the girl because she is always trying to polish the apple with her teacher.

- **rotten to the core** : to be completely worthless (like a rotten apple)

  ex) The political organization was rotten to the core and everybody knew that they must change.

- **upset the applecart** : to ruin a plan or event by surprise or accident

  ex) Everything was going well at the company picnic until our boss arrived and upset the applecart.

2. Bean Idioms

- **full of beans** : to feel energetic, to be in high spirits

  ex) My aunt is full of beans tonight and she does not want to stop talking.

- **not know beans about (someone or something)** : to know nothing about someone or something

  ex) I do not know beans about repairing a car.

- **not worth a hill of beans** : worthless

  ex) The man is a liar and what he says is not worth a hill of beans.

- **spill the beans** : to tell a secret to someone who is not supposed to know about it

  ex) "Please do not spill the beans about my plans to quit work and return to school next year."

3. Bread Idioms

- **as warm as toast** : very warm and cozy

  ex) Our house was as warm as toast when we went in from the rain.

- **bread and butter** : one's income/job to buy the basic needs of life like food/shelter/clothing

  ex) The voters are worried about bread-and-butter issues like jobs and taxes.

- **bread and water** : the most basic meal that is possible (just as you would get in prison)

  ex) The prisoners were fed bread and water for several days last winter.

- **greatest thing since sliced bread** : the greatest thing that there has ever been

  ex) My mother believes that the microwave oven is the greatest thing since sliced bread.

- **grist for the mill** : something that can be used to bring advantage or profit

  ex) The information that we got on the Internet was grist for the mill of our company's operations.

- **half a loaf is better than none** : a proverb that says that having part of something is better than having nothing at all

  ex) Half a loaf is better than none and I would rather work part-time than have no job at all.

- **half-baked** : to be not thought about or studied carefully

  ex) Our friend has a half-baked idea about starting a new business but most of us think that it will fail.

- **know which side one' s bread is buttered** : to know what is most advantageous for you

  ex) My aunt knows which side her bread is buttered when she visits her sister.

4. Cake Idioms

- **eat one' s cake and have it too** : to use or spend something and still keep it, to have something both ways

  ex) The man refuses to give up anything and he always wants to eat his cake and have it too.

- **have one' s cake and eat it too** : to use or spend something and still keep it, to have something both ways

  ex) I wanted to have my cake and eat it too when I wanted more holidays and more responsibility at work.

- **icing on the cake** : something that makes a good situation or activity even better

  ex) I was able to find a good job and the fact that I can work where I want is the icing on the cake.

- **piece of cake** : a task that is easily accomplished

  ex) The small job was a piece of cake. I had everything done before lunch this morning.

- **a slice of the cake** : a share of something

  ex) The government wants a slice of the cake of the money from the new casinos.

- **take the cake** : to be the best or worst of something

  ex) The behavior of the young girl takes the cake. It is terrible.

5. Cooking Idioms

- **as black as a skillet** : very black

  ex) The bottom of the little boy's feet were as black as a skillet.

- **burn(something) to a crisp** : to burn something very badly

  ex) I burned the eggs to a crisp when I left the stove on while I was talking on the telephone.

- **cook (someone's) goose** : to damage or ruin someone

  ex) I think that I cooked my goose when I made a mistake at work today.

- **cook(something) to perfection** : to cook something perfectly

  ex) The chef always cooks the food to perfection at the small restaurant.

- **cook(something) up** : to cook something, to make some kind of plan

  ex) I do not know what my girlfriend is cooking up for the weekend but we will probably do something interesting.

- **done to a T/turn** : to be cooked just right (just as one would cook a steak perfectly)

  ex) The steaks were done to a T when my friend cooked them on the barbecue.

- **(one' s) goose is cooked** : one has been found out and is now in trouble

  ex) I told a lie to my company and now my goose is cooked and I am in much trouble.

- **out of the frying pan and into the fire** : to go from something bad to something worse

  ex) The woman jumped out of the frying pan and into the fire when she quit her job. Now her problems are much worse.

- **too many cooks spoil the broth** : too many people trying to do something will cause problems

  ex) Too many cooks spoil the broth and we decided to have less people work on the project because having too many people was making it difficult to do anything.

- **toss a salad** : to mix a salad with the dressing

  ex) I quickly tossed a salad and we ate dinner.

6. Drink Idioms

- **Bottoms up!** : everybody should drink now (this expression is used at the end of a drinking toast)

  ex) "Bottoms up," our host said at the beginning of the dinner.

- **coffee break** : a break from work to rest and drink coffee/tea

  ex) We usually have a coffee break every morning at 10 o'clock.

- **cry over spilled/spilt milk** : to cry or complain about something that has already happened

  ex) You should not cry over spilled milk. The past is past and you cannot do anything to change it.

- **(not one's) cup of tea** : something that one does not enjoy or do well (usually used in the negative)

  ex) Going to art galleries is not my cup of tea so I think that I will stay home this evening.

- **down the hatch** : something is swallowed

  ex) My drink was down the hatch before I could order another one.

- **have a pick-me-up** : to eat or drink something stimulating

  ex) I wanted to have a pick-me-up so I stopped at a small shop for a coffee.

- **Here's mud in your eye!** : Drink up! (a drinking toast)

  ex) "Here's mud in your eye," I said as we drank a toast to my new job.

- **hit the sauce** : to drink alcohol (usually regularly)

  ex) I think that the woman began to hit the sauce after her husband lost his job.

- **milk of human kindness** : the natural kindness and sympathy that is shown to others

  ex) The woman at the community center is full of the milk of human kindness.

- **milk (someone) for (something)** : to pressure someone into giving information or money

  ex) The man was trying to milk the elderly lady for much of her money.

- **not for all the tea in China** : not for anything

  ex) I will not for all the tea in China lend my friend any more money.

- **wine and dine (someone)** : to treat someone to an expensive meal, to entertain someone in a lavish manner

  ex) My uncle often has to wine and dine his important business clients.

7. Egg Idioms

- **bad egg** : a bad person, a bum

  ex) My neighbor is a bad egg and you should avoid him if you can.

- **egg (someone) on** : to encourage someone to do something (often something bad/wrong/dangerous)

  ex) The boys egged their friend on to jump into the water.

- **good egg** : a good person

  ex) The man is a good egg and everybody likes him a lot.

- **have egg on one's face** : to be embarrassed (because of an obvious error)

  ex) The man has egg on his face now that he has admitted that he was wrong about his boss.

- **lay an egg** : to give a bad performance of something

  ex) The singer laid an egg during her performance last evening.

- **put all one's eggs in one basket** : to risk everything at once

  ex) I do not want to put all my eggs in one basket and only invest money in real estate.

- **teach one's grandmother to suck eggs** : to try to tell someone who has more knowledge than you how to do something

  ex) I tried to teach my friend something about computers but he is a computer expert. It was like teaching my grandmother to suck eggs.

- **walk on eggs** : to be very cautious

  ex) I must walk on eggs when I ask my friend to do something for me.

- **you can' t make an omelette without breaking the eggs** : you cannot do something without causing some problems or having some effects

  ex) "You can't make an omelette without breaking the eggs and if you want to change the work schedules, then you are going to cause problems."

8. Fish Idioms

- **fine kettle of fish** : a mess, an unsatisfactory situation

  ex) It was a fine kettle of fish that I was in when I lost the keys to my apartment.

- **have bigger fish to fry** : to have other more important things to do

  ex) I have bigger fish to fry and I do not want to spend every evening doing extra work for my company.

- **neither fish nor fowl** : not in any recognizable category

  ex) The movie was neither fish nor fowl and I did not know what category to put it into.

- **packed in like sardines** : to be packed in very tightly

  ex) The commuters were packed in like sardines in the subway car.

9. Fruit Idioms

- **as nutty as a fruitcake** : silly, crazy

  ex) The man in the supermarket was as nutty as a fruitcake.

- **bear fruit** : to yield or give results

  ex) The woman's hard work at her business finally began to bear fruit when she started to make money.

- **forbidden fruit** : something that one finds attractive partly because it is illegal/immoral/prohibited

  ex) Entering the old building was forbidden fruit for the young boys.

- **fruits of one' s labor** : the results of one's work

  ex) My father is retired now and he is finally enjoying the fruits of his labor.

10. Nut Idioms

- **everything from soup to nuts** : almost everything that one can think of

  ex) We brought everything from soup to nuts for our weekend holiday.

- for peanuts : for very little money, for almost nothing

  ex) I was able to buy a used computer for peanuts.

- hard nut to crack : a difficult person or thing to deal with

  ex) My friend is a very serious person and she is a very hard nut to crack.

- in a nutshell : briefly, in a few words

  ex) We went to the meeting and they told us in a nutshell about the plans for our company.

11. Pie Idioms

- **as easy as apple pie** : very easy

  ex) The test that I wrote yesterday was as easy as apple pie.

- **eat humble pie** : to be humbled, to admit one's error and apologize

  ex) Our boss was forced to eat humble pie after he made the wrong budget estimate for next year.

- **have one' s finger in the pie** : to be involved in something

  ex) The man has his finger in the pie of everything at his workplace.

- **have one' s finger in too many pies** : to be involved in too many things so that you cannot do any of them well

  ex) Our supervisor has her finger in too many pies to really do her job well.

- **pie in the sky** : an idea or plan that you think will never happen

  ex) My cousin's plans are usually pie in the sky and will never happen.

- **slice of the pie** : a share of something

  ex) The government wants a slice of the pie of the money from the new casinos.

12. Potato Idioms

- **couch potato** : someone who spends a lot of time on a couch watching television

  ex) My cousin is a couch potato and he never wants to leave his house.

- **drop (someone/something) like a hot potato** : to suddenly stop being involved with someone or with some kind of a problem

  ex) The advertisers dropped the basketball star like a hot potato when he became involved in a scandal.

- **hot potato** : a question or argument that is controversial and difficult to settle

  ex) The issue of building the nuclear power plant is a hot potato for the local town council.

- **meat and potatoes** : basic simple and good food, simple tastes

ex) The man is a meat-and-potatoes person who enjoys the simple pleasures of life.

- **small potatoes** : something that is not very big or important compared with other things or people

  ex) The amount of money for the stadium is small potatoes compared to the total cost of the Olympics.

13. Salt Idioms

- **back to the salt mines** : to go back to work (this is a humorous expression to express going back to unpleasant work)

  ex) "Lunch is over so let's go back to the salt mines for the afternoon."

- **rub salt in (someone' s) wound** : to try to make someone's unhappiness or misfortune worse

  ex) I did not mention the car accident to my friend because I did not want to rub salt in his wound.

- **salt of the earth** : good/basic/honest/ordinary people

  ex) Our new neighbors are the salt of the earth. They are good, basic, honest people.

- **salt (something) away** : to save money or some other item

  ex) I am salting away much money from my new job.

- **take (something) with a grain of salt** : to accept or believe something with much doubt, to not give much credit or importance to something that was said

  ex) "You should take everything that the supervisor says with a grain of salt because he likes to exaggerate things."

- **worth one' s salt** : to be a good worker, to be worth what one is paid

  ex) The man has only been working here for a month but quickly he is proving that he is worth his salt.

14. Soup Idioms

- **as easy as duck soup** : very easy

  ex) It was as easy as duck soup to find the book that I wanted in the library.

- **as thick as pea soup** : very thick (can be used with fog as well as with liquids)

  ex) The fog was as thick as pea soup when we walked along the beach.

- **duck soup** : a task that does not require much effort

  ex) "It was like duck soup. I was able to finish my school project last night."

- **everything from soup to nuts** : almost everything that one can think of

  ex) We brought everything from soup to nuts for our weekend holiday.

- **in the soup** : in serious trouble, in a bad situation

  ex) The woman is in the soup now. She told her boss that she was sick but he saw her downtown shopping.

- **soup up (something)** : to make something faster or more powerful by changing or adding something (this expression is often used for a car)

  ex) My neighbor decided to soup up the car that he recently bought.

- **too many cooks spoil the broth** : too many people trying to do something will cause problems

  ex) Too many cooks spoil the broth and we decided to have less people work on the project because having too many people was making it difficult to do anything.

15. Stew Idioms

- **get oneself into a stew over (someone or something)** : to be worried or upset about someone or something

  ex) I try hard not to get myself into a stew over some of the rude remarks of my supervisor.

- **in a stew about/over (someone or something)** : to be worried or upset about someone or something

  ex) My father is in a stew over the fact that his order of car parts has not arrived.

- **stew in one s own juice** : to suffer from something that you yourself have caused to happen

  ex) The man is the one who caused the problem for himself and he is now being forced to stew in his own juice.

- **too many cooks spoil the stew** : too many people trying to do something will cause problems

  ex) Too many cooks spoil the broth and we decided to have less people work on the project because having too many people was making it difficult to do anything.

N.o.t.e

-polish : to make (something) smooth and shiny by rubbing

-flatter : to make (someone) feel important or attractive, or to praise (someone) in order to please them

-core : the center or most important part of something

-grist : grain that is ground into flour

-hatch : an opening through a wall, floor, etc., or the cover for it:

-lavish : more than enough, especially if expensive; very generous

-bum : someone who has no home or job and lives by asking other people for money

-suck : to pull in liquid or air through your mouth without using your teeth, or to move the tongue and muscles of the mouth around something inside your mouth, often in order to dissolve it

-sardine : a small sea fish which can be eaten

-exaggerate : to make something seem larger, more important, better or worse than it really is

R.e.f.e.r.n.c.e.s

http://www.idiomconnection.com/food.html

http://dictionary.cambridge.org/

http://en.wikipedia.org/wiki/

http://encarta.msn.com/encnet/features/dictionary/

http://www.merriam-webster.com/

http://www.onelook.com/

Chapter 10 True/ False Quizzes for Food Safety in the Kitchen

1. Food Safety Quiz for Cold Food

The importance of keeping cold food cold is the focus of Food Safety Month. Food safety experts remind us to use proper refrigeration and prompt cooling techniques to protect food from harmful bacteria.

How much do you know about cold food storage, handling and preparation? Take this quick true-false quiz to determine your Cool IQ.

1) True or False?

① Refrigeration prevents bacterial growth.

② The refrigerator temperature should be set at 40° F and the freezer temperature should be set at 0° F.

③ The best method to thaw food is at room temperature.

④ The refrigerator should be tightly packed with food and containers to keep items cold.

⑤ A refrigerator/freezer thermometer is the best tool to check and monitor the temperature inside the refrigerator and freezer compartments.

⑥ Perishables, prepared foods and leftovers need to be refrigerated or frozen within 5 hours of purchase or preparation.

⑦ To thaw quickly, it's best to submerge food in cold water in airtight packaging, or thaw food in the microwave and cook immediately.

⑧ Always marinate foods in the refrigerator.

⑨ Hot foods should be placed directly in the refrigerator.

⑩ When traveling, stow the cooler with perishable food in the trunk to avoid the sunlight and added heat.

N.o.t.e

–thaw : to (cause to) change from a solid, frozen state to a liquid or soft one, because of an increase in temperature

–perishables : items of food that decay quickly

–stow : to store something

Answers

GUIDE TO KITCHEN ENGLISH

Let's see how you did.

① **False.**

Refrigeration slows, but does not prevent growth of harmful bacteria. Always remember to refrigerate food quickly!

② **True.**

③ **False.**

Always defrost food in the refrigerator. This is the safest method for all foods. Use the microwave to defrost food only if it will be cooked immediately. To quickly thaw meat and poultry in airtight packaging, submerge frozen package into cold water. Change the water every 30 minutes, so the meat continues to thaw.

④ **False.**

Don't overfill the refrigerator. Cold air must be able to circulate inside the refrigerator to keep food cold and safe. Remove clutter from the refrigerator on a routine basis.

⑤ **True.**

Thermometers are valuable kitchen tools. Check the temperature of the refrigerator on a regular basis using a refrigerator/freezer thermometer.

⑥ False.

Perishables, prepared food and leftovers need to be refrigerated or frozen within 2 hours of purchase or preparation, and if the temperature is above 90°F, foods should not be left out for longer than an hour.

⑦ True.

⑧ True.

⑨ True.

But, divide large quantities of food into shallow containers for quicker cooling.

⑩ False.

Travel with the cooler stored in the coolest part of the car. The trunk is usually one of the hottest spots because of lack of ventilation.

2. Food Safety Quiz in Cooking

Let's see how much you learn about food safety in cooking. Please answer the questions below. Good luck!

1) True or False?

① Since the food is going to be cooked, I don' t need to wash my hands before starting the food preparation.

② It is okay to sample food before it is fully cooked to see if it is okay.

③ I should never use the same cutting board, utensils and plates for raw meats and other foods.

④ Since the kitchen counter is warmer it is better to thaw meats on the counter instead of the refrigerator.

⑤ You should always pick up perishables last when shopping and refrigerate them as soon as possible.

⑥ You should allow more time when cooking something that is frozen.

⑦ Bacteria grow rapidly at ordinary room temperatures.

⑧ You can tell meat is done by the color it is inside.

⑨ You should use large containers for storing food.

⑩ When in doubt, throw it out.

N.o.t.e

-sample : to taste a small amount of food or drink to decide whether you like it

Answers

Let's see how you did.

① False.

Always wash your hands before beginning food preparation. Also, try not to sneeze or cough into the food. If you sneeze or cough, wash your hands again.

② False.

Tasting raw meat, poultry and other foods can make you sick. Make sure you wash fruits and vegetables and cook meats and eggs. It is also important not to taste food that looks or smells bad to see if you can still use it. Just discard it.

③ True.

Use a separate cutting board for meats or thoroughly wash the cutting board, utensils, counter and your hands before continuing in the food preparation.

④ False.

There are three correct ways to thaw meat, either in the refrigerator, in the microwave or under cold running water.

⑤ True.

It is very important that perishable food is never left out of the refrigerator for more than 2 hours.

⑥ True.

At least 1 ~ 1 ½ additional hours should be allowed for cooking frozen foods.

⑦ True.

Bacteria grow quickly and rapidly at room temperature. Make sure food is not left out for over 2 hours and use a thermometer to check your refrigerator and freezer to see if they are at the proper temperatures.

⑧ False.

The color of meat and poultry is not a sure sign of its doneness. Some foods, especially smoked poultry, remains pink no matter how long you cook it. Only by using a food thermometer can you determine if the food is done.

⑨ False.

When storing leftovers you should use small, shallow containers and refrigerate them immediately.

⑩ True.

R.e.f.e.r.n.c.e.s

http://www.mass.gov/dph/cdc/epii/foodsafety/foodsafetyquiz.htm

http://www.vdacs.virginia.gov/foodsafety/refrigquiz.shtml

http://dictionary.cambridge.org/

http://www.merriam-webster.com/

http://www.onelook.com/

Chapter 11 Crossword Puzzle and Word Puzzle

Here are two crossword puzzles and one word puzzle based on kitchen, restaurant, and food. Let's enjoy playing with words.

1. Kitchen Crossword

Across

4. What do you eat soup in?
7. What do you slice bread with?
9. Where do you fry eggs?
10. What do many Asians use to eat food?
11. What do you make soup in?
13. What do you make lemonade in?
14. Where do you keep milk cold?
16. Where do you keep meat frozen?

Down

1. Where do you heat pots and pans?
2. What do you eat soup with?
3. What do you drink water from?
5. Where do you wash dishes?
6. Where do you keep cups, glasses, plates, and bowls?
8. What do you keep ketchup in?
10. What do you pour coffee into?
12. What do you serve food on?
13. What do you keep jam in?
15. Where do you bake bread?

2. Restaurants and Food Crossword

Across

2. Someone who makes food in a cheap restaurant. (4)
4. A meal between breakfast and lunch. (6)
5. Someone who makes food in an expensive restaurant. (4)
8. This describes what you can eat at a restaurant. (4)
11. Something you eat before the main meal. (9)
12. If everybody pays for their own food then you go ________. (5)
13. A side dish with lettuce and other vegetables. (5)
15. What the cook places your food on. (5)

16. A meal where you help yourself from a table with a variety of dishes. (6)
17. Long, stringy food. (7)
18. Something you give your waiter if the service is good. (3)

Down

1. A place where people can sit around and drink alcoholic beverages in a restaurant.(3)
2. A drink that many people have with dessert. (6)
3. Something you use to cut meat. (5)
4. Another word for a drink. (8)
6. The noon meal. (5)
7. Something you might need to get into a busy restaurant. (11)
9. Someone who serves you food. (6)
10. The morning meal. (9)
12. Something, usually sweet, that you eat after dinner. (7)
14. The evening meal (6)
16. The total amount that you have to pay for a meal. (4)

3. Kitchen Word Search

G K H P S R E I G V S G E Y A N
J A R L L E D X H S U M D D D B
P D G Q V A H E A V N L B Q F W
Y E F O B N T L A S A X C O S V
S C T O D F G E C U U R A I W O
C S V B V F P M U X K W N L C L
Y W Y R G R W V P K F W I L O K
Q W S O N I I H B J C T E A U L
J W J U R D Q N O B O F M Z N V
U F L U Z G B D A P O V F P T D
N A I C G E Z B R X L T D P E B
B C P T U G I F D M O L T N R V
Z A O E F T L S R P E N O L L S
Z N S K S I N K U L B O X X E C
H K R K A B Z C B H P I L I M H
K O P X E P T A V S T Z B C D A
F F B A S T T S Q K M S Y U O I
N H M K N X H V M K N I F E W R

Find all of the kitchen words below in the grid.

bottle, bowl, box, can, chair, counter, cup, cupboard, fork, fridge, glass, jar, jug, knife, pan, plate, pot, sink, spoon, stove, table

R.e.f.e.r.n.c.e.s

http://bogglesworldesl.com/ox/restaurant_crossword.doc

Guide to Kitchen Enlgish

Part Ⅲ
Speaking

Guide to Kitchen English

Chapter 12 Level one

1. Greetings

Good morning/afternoon/evening/night.

Hi.(Hello.) / How are you? / How are you doing?

Fine. How about you? Okay. Thanks.

How do you do, Mr. Jefferson?

I'm glad (pleased / honored) to meet you

I've heard a lot about you.

I've been wanting to meet you for along time.

Have a good (or nice) day/weekend.

How have you been? / How have you been doing?

/ How have things been?

I haven't seen you for a long time. / I haven't seen you in years.

I haven't seen you for ages.

Hi, long time no see.

It's been a long time, hasn't it? / It's been months, hasn't it?

It's been quite a while, hasn't it?

I'm glad to see you again. / Glad to see you.

It's nice (or good) to see you again.

2. Introduce Yourself

I'm Mary. (Use first name in informal situations)

I'm Mary Sullivan. (Use full name in business and formal situations)

(It's) nice to meet you. / (It's) nice meeting you. / (It's) good to meet you.

Nice to meet you too. / I'm pleased to meet you. / I'm glad to meet you, too.

3. Introduce Kitchen Staff members

This is my friend, Jeff/my boss, Mr. Johnson / my co-worker, William Taylor.

Hi Jack. I'm Maria

Nice to meet you. / Nice to meet you too.

4. Identify People and Things

This is Alfred Parker. / That is Mr. Carroll.

Mr. Adams is a head cook / a foodstylist / a line cook / a certified master chef.

We are cooks. / They are waiters.

This is an apple / a banana / an orange.

That is not a tomato. / It is a pimento / a pomegranate.

What is your name? My name is Robert. / You can call me Bob.

What is it? That's(It's) a corkscrew.

What is that? It's a rolling pin.

How do you say it in English? Fridge.

How do you spell it? F-R-I-D-G-E

Please say it again. All right.

Please speak more slowly. OK. Listen carefully.

I don't understand. Let me explain.

I'm sorry. That's O.K.(okay).

5. Ask for Information

What is this? This(It) is a blender

What is that? That(It) is a mincer.

What are these? These(They) are slicers.

What are those? Those(They) are saucepans.

Where is Chef Edward? He is over there.

Where's William? He's in the kitchen.

When's the meeting? It's at 9:00.

When's lunch? Lunch is at noon.

How is the food? It's delicious.

What are your work hours? My work hours are from 9 to 5.

What are your work days? My work days are from Monday to Friday.

What is your schedule for tomorrow? I have meeting on menu design all day.

6. Giving Information

Kelly is from Oregon. Oh really?

What part of Oregon? Coos bay.

Jane is a restaurant manager. Is that right?

What restaurant? Bill's.

He's a College student.

Oh. What College? Hyejeon.

Randy works in Korea. Really? What city (in Korea)? Seoul.

I work at a restaurant. Oh really? Which restaurant? Angelo Meroni's

Where are you from? I'm from San Francisco.

What is your occupation? I'm a Kitchen Manager.

7. Simple Sentences

I work in Sardi's. Are you a waiter? No, I'm a head cook.

Greg works in Tom's Restaurant . Is he an owner? Yes, he is.

They live in Washington. Are they cooks? No, they aren't.

I eat breakfast at 8:00 a.m. What do you eat? (I eat) eggs, bacon, and toast.

She goes to work at 10:00 a.m. Where does she work? In the kitchen.

I don't drink beer. Why (not)? I don't like it.

8. Simple Questions

1) Very Simple (Yes/No Questions)

Are chefs artists? Yes, they are.

Is he a cook? No, he isn't.

Is great cooking really art? Yes, it is.

Is this a salamander? Yes, it is.

Do you like cooking? Yes, I do.

2) More examples (Yes/No Questions)

Is she going to the meeting? Yes, she is.

Are they flying home? No, they're taking the bus.

Are you coming to the party? No, I have other plans.

Does she work in Hard Rock Cafe International? No, she doesn't

Do you live close to public transportation? No, I don't

Do you eat a big or small breakfast?

Do you have a recipe for sausage soup?

Do you have a chef in mind?

3) Examples of simple Wh—questions

What are the five mother sauces?

What do you do (as an occupation)? I'm a cook.

What do you do on the weekends? I usually stay home and watch television.

Why are you late for work?

How do you say that in English?

How do you spell this dried ingredient? I'm not sure, but R-O-S-E-M-A-R-Y.

9. Number and Counting

How many chefs in your kitchen? Thirty-five, including me.

How many waitpersons in your floor?

How old is your chef? She is twenty-nine.

How many hours do you work every day? From nine to five. Eight hours.

How many cooks are in the group? About seven.

How many cookies are left? Five or six.

How many toothpicks are in the box? More than a hundred.

How many potatoes do you peel? I peel about 3 sacks of potatoes every day.

How much annual leave or sick leave does your company grant?

How many days of annual leave or sick leave can you use every year?

What is the monthly number of patrons at the restaurant?

What is the average annual revenues for the restaurant?

When did the restaurant open?

What is the average salary a sous chef earns in Korea?

How long have you been cooking professionally?

How much does a chef make in a year? A chef's salary varies by position and location.

What is the distance from the exit No.2 of Sadang station on the green line to the restaurant site?

10. Talking about company

This is my employer/boss. He is an owner and chef. These are my co-workers.

There are ten cooks in the kitchen.

Does your company provide transportation?

Does your company provide food ?

The restaurant employs approximately 10 people.

Most employees are paid by the hour.

My restaurant is the best place to work.

Every employee has to attend a training course every summer.

What are your work hours like?

What is the theme of the restaurant?

What types of food are served at the restaurant?

This two-story building is located on the western part of Hoseong.

My restaurant is a two-story building. The ground floor is occupied by the restaurant, the second floor by a deli and liquor store.

The success of my restaurant is built on the highest standards of quality, service and cleanliness delivered to customers.

My primary responsibility is to prepare the food, serve customers, and carry out tasks for the efficient running of the restaurant.

11. Talking about Favourite Things

What is your favorite food / season / sport / subject / number / snack?

What's your favorite kind of music?

Do you have a lucky number?

What kind of food do you like best? I like Cantonese food.

Who is your favorite chef/relative/movie star/singer?

What city do you like most? Hong Kong, of course!

What do you enjoy most about your profession?

12. Talking about Here and Now

What is Ms. Chan doing? She is mopping floors. Oh. That's nice.

What is he doing? He's cleaning burners. That's interesting.

What are you doing? I'm making stock. Is it interesting?

Who is peeling that carrot? Frank (is). Oh. It looks good.

Who is doing the dishes? The trainees are. That's great.

Where are you going now? I'm going to the kitchen.
Okay. Good work.

13. Talking about Feelings/Health Issues

How's the weather today?
It's nice / good / beautiful / warm / cold / chilly / windy / wonderful.

How're you getting along these days?

How do you feel? / How are you feeling? / How's every little thing?

How's everything with you? / How's business? / How's it going?

How're things going? / How goes it? / Is everything okay(right)?

What's new? / What's wrong? / What's the matter? / Are you all right?

Not too good. / I'm fine. / Great! / Couldn't be better. / The same.

Could be better. / Okay, I suppose. / Just okay. / Things are fine.

Fine, thanks. / I feel sick. / I have a headache.

My leg hurts. / I cut my hand / My finger caught the blade.

14. Telling Time

It's five o'clock.	It's five p.m. / a.m.
It's twelve o'clock.	It's noon / midnight.
It's four ten.	It's ten (minutes) after four.
It's five fourteen.	It's fourteen after five.
It's six fifteen.	It's (a) quarter after six.
It's one twenty-one	It's twenty-one minutes past one.
It's eleven oh five.	It's five after eleven.
It's two oh nine.	It's nine minutes past two.

It's six thirty. It's half past six.

It's three fifty. It's ten minutes to four.

It's ten forty-five. It's quarter to eleven.

It's eight thirty-five. It's twenty-five minutes to nine.

It's a few minutes before four.

15. Talking about Past Actions

What happened? He broke his arm. Call 911!

When did you get off work? I got off work at 5:30.

What did Sally have for lunch? She had soup and sandwiches.

How was the weather? It was wonderful.

Were you educated here? No. I wasn't.

Did Sam grow up here? Yes, he did.

Did you enjoy the korean cuisine?" "Yes, I enjoyed it very much."

Where did you do your training?

What was your first restaurant job?

What was your worst kitchen disaster?

Did you enjoy the movie? Yes, I did.

Did you pay the phone bill?

Did you catch the second episode of Next Iron Chef last night?

Where else did you go besides California?

How did you do on your exam?

Did you make an appointment to see your adviser?

Who did it?

Who did you work with?

I dreamed I won a million dollars.

Due to the bad weather the contest was cancelled.

There was an earthquake last night.

The vice president was elevated to president.

We were elevated by the beautiful weather.

He didn't have food and nutrition, but he had an English class.

She didn't offer me even a cup of tea.

Whose knife did you borrow?

What kind of soup did you make?

16. Talking about the Future (will vs. "be going to" + verb)

1) will

What will you do tomorrow? I'll clean the kitchen.

What time will the pasta be ready? In twenty minutes.

How will he get there? He'll take the bus.

Where will you work after graduation? I'll work for The Four Seasons.

Will the train on time?

I'll be at the office between nine and eleven.

Do you think it will rain? It won't rain.

I will be happy when this is finished.

This time tomorrow I'll be sitting in the sun.

He'll have finished the whole job by this evening.

"There's somebody coming up the stairs." "That'll be Mary."

"Can somebody help me?" "I'll."

"There's door bell." "I'll go."

Where will he be next week?

He'll leave for the airport at four o'clock.

I'll do the dishes/the salad.

She will continue as principal of the school.

2) "be going to" + verb.

What are you going to do first? We're going to blanch the bones.

What is he going to do? He's going to study in France next year.

I'm going to make an appointment for an interview right now.

Look at the sky. It's going to rain.

17. Expressing Likes and Dislikes

What does James like? (What are his personal preferences?)

He likes horror movies/basketball / chocolate ice cream.

I like you so much/very much. I like it fine.

I like you and your sister very much.

"Do you like fishing?" "Yes I do."

Do you like to walk in the woods alone?

Which do you like better coffee or tea?

I like(love) to see her everyday.

I don't like to drink at home by myself.

I like playing tennis.

"How do you like your egg?" "I like it boiled."

I like my coffee sweet.

What would you like for breakfast?

I'd like bacon and eggs, biscuits, and coffee.

"Can I go now?" "If you like."

Do it the way you like to.

Come when you like.

You can sit whenever you like.

They have hated each other since high school.

I hate mice!/you!

Mother hated to move from such a nice town.

I hate to interrupt you.

18. Closing a Conversation

1) Before closing

It's been nice talking to you. Nice talking to you too.

(I'm sorry, but) I have to go now.

The host of the talk show always closed by saying,

"Good-bye until next time."

The announcer always ended by saying,

"Be with us again next week at this time. Good-bye until then."

2) Closing

Good-bye. Bye. See you later/soon. See ya. (informal)
Catch you later. (informal)

19. Expressing Thanks

Thanks. / Many thanks. / Thank you. / Thank you so much(very much).
Thanks for the tour. your time.
Thank you for the nice gift. Thank god, the bus is finally here.
I'm extremely thankful to him for his help.
I appreciate it / that / your kindness. It would be highly appreciated.
I do appreciate what you have done for me.
Yes, his work was highly appreciated by all of us.

N.o.t.e

–pimento (US USUALLY pimiento) : a sweet red pepper

–pomegranate : a round thick-skinned fruit containing a mass of red juicy seeds

–mop : to use a mop to wash something

R.e.f.e.r.n.c.e.s

http://bogglesworldesl.com/

http://dictionary.cambridge.org/

http://en.wikipedia.org/wiki/

http://encarta.msn.com/encnet/features/dictionary/

http://fpcctalkindian.nativeweb.org/nles3.htm

http://free-english-study.com/speaking/

http://starchefs.com/experts/chefs/

http://www.english-grammar-lessons.com/

http://www.englishgrammarsecrets.com/index.html

http://www.learn-english-today.com/free-english-lessons/

http://www.merriam-webster.com/

http://www.myenglishzone.com/

http://www.onelook.com/

Chapter 13 Level Two

1. American Numbers and Prices

1) Remember that in English, we divide prices at the decimal point.

For example : $4.59 our dollars (and) fifty-nine cents (long way)
four / fifty nine (short way)

(Time is also divided in a similar way : 12:47 is said "twelve / forty-seven")

$1.79* *Also: a dollar seventy-nine

$29.00** **Also: twenty-nine (dollars) even

That will be 16 dollars 40 cents. That comes to 100 dollars.

Your bill comes to $15.99.

2) Americans often say large numbers in "phrases" of two digits.

For example: 267 two hundred sixty-seven (long way)
two / sixty seven (short way)

4,381 four thousand three hundred eighty-one (long way)
forty-three / eighty-one (short way)

3) Some people also use two-digit phrasing with telephone numbers :

565-8347 five-six-five // eighty-three / forty-seven

2. Simple Shopping

shop around / shop-keepe / shop-lifter
shopping-bag / shopping-center / eye shopping

There are many new shops at the new building.
I shop at a supermarket near my home.
I'm shopping for a new dishwasher.
I'm shopping around for reduced rates.
Give me a ballpark figure.
Did she get lost on the tenth floor?
It's the very thing that I've been looking for.
Every items are on half price sale.
Where can I get a bottle opener?
How much is a basket of apples? It's $19.95. Okay. I'll take it.
How much does this cost? That one is $5.00. How about this one?
How much does it go for?
That comes to $26.59. Here's $30.00. Your change is $3.41
That will be $17.48. Here's $17.50. Keep the change. Thanks.

3. Making Suggestions

I think you should eat something light before going to work.

That's a good idea.

I don't think you should work the night shift.

Thanks for the advice, but I really need the money.

Let's go bowling tonight.

Sorry, I can't. I'm going to meet a friend for dinner.

Why don't we go skiing on Saturday?

Sounds like a good idea. Where do you want to go?

Why don't you come with me to China?

Thanks, but I've already been there.

4. Asking for Favors

Can you help me with my math?

Sure. What's the problem?

Could you bring me some coffee?

I'd be glad to. How do you like it?

Would you open the door for me?

No problem. It looks like your hands are full.

Could I ask you a favor?

It depends. What is it?

5. Asking for Repetition

Would you speak slowly, please?

Say it again please.

Would you spell out your name, please?

Yes, my name is Mr. Smith. S as in Sam. M as in Marry.

I as in ice. T as in tomato. H as in happy.

What did you say your name was?

It's Cathy Henderson.

Did you say Andersen or Henderson?

Henderson, with an H.

Is "Cathy" spelled with a C or a K?

It's C as in Cadillac.

Sorry, I didn't catch the last part.

Do you want me to repeat it?

I can't hear you very well.

Maybe you should turn down the radio.

6. Requesting

Pass the bread.   Here you are.

Please buy the pepper for me.

Okay. I'll stop by the grocery store on my way to work.

Would you please turn down the heat to about medium?

Sorry. Is it hot for you?

Will you print my Monday to Friday schedule for me?

Sure. When do you need it?

Would you give me a ride to work?

Sorry. I'm not going in that direction.

7. Offering

Here. Have a cookie.

Thanks.

Would you like some pie?

No thank you. It looks delicious though.

How about a glass of wine?

Thanks, but I don't drink (alcohol).

What will you have (to drink)?

Orange juice will be fine.

Would you like some more cake?

Sure. It's really good. Did you bake it yourself?

Can I get you some milk or something?

Well, a glass of water would be okay.

8. Talking about Abilities

Can you peel a cucumber?

Yes, but not very well.

How about the guitar?

(I can play) a little.

Can Billy ride a snowboard?

No, he can't. He's too old.

Does Abby speak Mandarin?

Yes, she speaks very well.

Do you sing?

Not really. I have no talent in that area.

Is Connie good at dancing?

Yes, she's a great dancer.

Do you know how to use an ice machine?

Of course!

9. Expressing Possibility

The manager may send him home.

She may be in California next Monday.

It might rain this afternoon.

You may be right.

"She didn't say hello." " She may not have recognized you."

I may see you tomorrow.

10. Talking about Locations

Where is the outlet? It is behind the refrigerator.

Where is the pestle and mortar? They're in the top drawer of cabinet.

Where's the strainer? It is over the grater.

Where's the strainer? It is under the working table.

Where is the bottle opener? It is on the lazy susan in the center of dining hall.

Where did you find the spatular? It was beneath the cutting board.

Where is the countertop? It is between the refrigerator and the stove.

Where is the cooktop? It is next to the refrigerator.

Where is Chef? He is in front of the ice machine.

Where is the dishpan? It is above the broiler.

Where is the lemon squeezer? It is below the coffee grinder.

Where is the scoop? It is inside the rice cooker.

Where's Donald? He's probably outside the kitchen.

11. Talking about Travel

How do you get to work? I usually take a commuter bus.

How long does it take? It takes an hour and a half.

How often do you drive your car? Once in a while.

Do you ever walk to work? No, that would take forever.

Are you going anywhere this summer? Probably to China.

How are you going to get there? By boat.

Why don't you fly? Airplane tickets are too expensive.

12. Describing People and things

1) Physical description

Age : about 20, in her thirties, nearly 50, very young, very old

Eye : green, blue, black,

Height : short, tall, fairly short, medium height, pretty tall, average

Hair : straight black, red long, curly, frizzy, blonde, short, brown, balding

Size : thin, overweight, chubby, big, fat, skinny

The way that someone looks or seems : gorgeous, nice, attractive, charming, handsome, ugly, stunning, be in good health, be a good looking guy,

wear glasses(pants, t-shirt, sneakers, make-up, a hat, socks, skirt, blouse, boots, dress, rings, earrings)

carry a purse(a bag, an umbrella, a camera, a cellphone, identification)

What does your mother look like?

What does Martha look like?

What does he look like?

What is your brother wearing?

What kind of shoes does he have (on)?

Is Susan wearing a dress?

What else can you tell me?

2) Description of personality

active, agreeable, ambitious, benevolent, cheerful, clever, cold-blooded, cold-hearted, communicative, compassionate, conservative, conscientious, considerate, cooperative, cruel, cunning, dishonest, easygoing, extrovert, frank, friendly, funny, flexible, generous, good-natured, greedy, hard-working, honest, hostile, hot-tempered, humane, humorous, ill-mannered, impolite, introvert, jealous, kind, lofty, mean, mischievous, modest, negative, negligent, open-minded, optimistic, outgoing, people-oriented, positive, practical, progressive, punctual, quiet, reliable, reserved, rude, ruthless, sensitive, selfish, smart, social, stern, strong, stubborn, sympathetic, suspicious, talkative, thoughtful, thoughtless, timid, unselfish, warm, warm-blooded, warlike, whole-hearted, withdrawn,

Tell me about your boss. What kind of person is he?

What is John like?

3) Description of things

Tell me about your new kitchen. Well, it's pretty small, but it's comfortable enough for me.

What did you think of the Himalayas? Well, the view was gorgeous. Of course, it took two days to get there, and the weather was freezing!

How would you describe your cooking style? Delicious and Healthy Cooking with Soul.

13. Like / Would like

What kind of food do you like? (Facts, personal preferences)

I like ice cream/bananas/soda pop/Italian food.

What kind of chef do you like?

I like someone who is easygoing. I like a person who has good looks.

I like people who are humorous.

What kind of food would you like? (If you could choose)

I would like Chinese food.

What kind of shift would you like?

I would like the day shift.

What kind of shift would you like to work?

I would like the night shift which has a lot of time.

14. Measure words

This can be used to practice countable nouns and uncountable nouns in context. When talking about uncountable items (such as sugar, water, toothpaste, etc.), it is common to use measure words to indicate how much of the substance you are referring to.

1) Food

A bag of flour / popcorn / chips / ice   A basket of grapes/mushroo

A bowl of rice/noodles, A box of cereal / chocolates / donuts / crackers / cookies,

A bucket of fish/chicken   A can of soup/peas/pop,

A carton of ice cream   A clove of garlic,

A crate of tomatoes/apples   A cube of ice

A dash of salt   A dish of spaghetti

An ear of corn   A grain of wheat/salt

A handful of peanuts/popcorn   A head of lettuce/cabbage

A jar of peanut butter/pickles/jam   A kernel of corn

A loaf of bread   A pack of gum

A package of pasta   A piece of cake/pie

A plate of french fries/cookies   A pound of meat/cheese

A sack of coconuts, potatoes   A slice of bread/pizza/cheese

A spear of asparagus   A stalk of celery

2) Liquid

A bottle of wine/water/ketchup/milk/soda/beer/ketchup

A bowl of soup/cereal

A carton of milk

A cup of coffee,

A drop of vinegar/medicine/rain

A gallon of punch

A glass of water

A half gallon of juice

A jug of lemonade

A keg of beer,

A liter of water

A pint of blood

A pot of coffee/soup

A quart of milk

A shot of vodka

A spoonful of sugar/medicine,

A tablespoon of vinegar

A tank of gas,

A teaspoon of medicine

3) Personal items

A ball of cotton

A bar of soap

A bottle of perfume/cologne

A carton of cigarettes

A container of shampoo

A roll of toilet paper

A stem of roses

A stick of deodorant

A tube of toothpaste

4) Sewing items

A skein of yarn

A spool of thread

A (square) foot/meter of fabric/cloth

A yard/meter of ribbon

5) Stationery

A bottle/tube of glue

A pad of paper

A piece of paper

A stick/piece of chalk

A jar of paste

A pair of scissors

A roll of tape

Remarks :

1) Measure words can also be counted: one slice of toast, two slices of toast, etc.

2) Some items can be either countable or uncountable, depending on composition or arrangement.

Below are a few examples of measure words used in English.

For example,

A bar of chocolate (uncountable [perceived as one solid item])
A box of chocolates (countable [perceived as several individual items])

15. Telephone Talk

Conversation 1

A : Hello. May I speak to Sarah?

B : Who's calling, please?

A : This is Robert speaking.

B : Just a moment, please. I will see if she is in.

A : Thank you.

B : Hello. I'm sorry. I have kept you waiting so long.

A : You're welcome.

B : She is not in the kitchen right now. Will you call her later on?

A : Certainly, I'll do. Thank you.

Conversation 2

A : Hello. May I speak to James, please?

B : I'm sorry, but he just stepped out. May I ask who's calling?

A : This is Kevin.

B : Kevin, Would you care to leave a message?

A : Yes. Please tell him that I called to discuss the new employment procedure with him.

B : All right. I'll tell him you called.

Conversation 3

A : Good afternoon, Susan speaking.

B : Hello, this is June. I'm returning your call.

A : Hello, June. I'm glad I got a hold of you.

B : What can I do for you?

A : Are you still looking for a part-time job?

B : Yes, I am.

Conversation 4

A : Hello, Richard. This is Julie. I want to return the cook book I borrowed from you last week. Will you be home today at about 5 o'clock?

B : Yes, I will. I'll be cooking dinner.

A : Oh, well. Then I won't come over at five.

B : Why not?

A : I don't want to disturb you. You'll be cooking dinner!

B : Don't worry. You won't disturb me.

A : O.K. I'll see you at five.

Conversation 5

A : Hi Gloria. This is Arthur. Can I come over and visit this evening?

B : No, Arthur. I'm afraid I won't be home this evening. I'll be shopping at the supermarket.

A : Can I come over and visit tomorrow evening?

B : No, Arthur. I'm afraid I won't be home tomorrow evening. I'll be working late at the office.

A : Can I come over and visit this weekend?

B : No, Arthur. I'll be visiting my sister in New York.

A : Can I come over and visit next Wednesday?

B : No, Arthur. I'll be visiting my uncle in the hospital.

A : How about some time next spring?

B : No, Arthur. I'll be getting married next spring.

A : Oh!

B : Good-bye.

16. Talking about Events during Lifelong Employment

When did you start working as a kitchen helper? In 1995.

Which restaurant did you work in? At Majung Restaurant.

Where did you work as a chef before? At Jihwaja Restaurant.

Did you ever attend any continuing education courses?

Yes, I did. In 2006, I attended the course of coffee barista offered by School of Continuing Education, Sookmyung Women's University last year.

Did you ever attend any executive education programs your company offers?

Yes, I did. In 2007, I attended the executive education program offered by Samsung Foodculture Division.

Did you ever use people in higher positions as mentors?

Yes, I did. I used Diana, line cook, as my mentor for 6 months in 1995. That was a big help to me.

Have you ever been awarded for your skills?

Yes, I've won four Gold Medals and the World Championship at the 1984 and 1988 Culinary Olympics in Germany.

How many times did you get awarded? I got awarded 8 times.

When was the last time you were promoted?

On December 29(th), 2004, I got promoted to Restaurant manager.

When did you earn Certified Master Chef (C.M.C.) status?

In Oct, 2005, I earned Certified Master Chef (C.M.C.) status from the ACF.

Did you ever serve as president for any organizations relative to culinary?

Yes, I served as ACF vice president.

When did you earn bachelor's degree?

In 1997, I earned my bachelor's degree in political science from Duke University.

When did you earn master's degree?

In 2001, I earned my master's degree in psychology from Georgetown University.

When did you earn your doctorate?

In 2007, I earned my doctorate in education from the University of Pennsylvania.

N.o.t.e

- **a ballpark figure** : This is a rough or approximate number (guesstimate) to give a general idea of something, like a rough estimate for a cost, etc.
- **frizzy** : (of hair) very curly and not smooth or shiny
- **balding** : becoming bald
- **chubby** : (especially of children) fat in a pleasant and attractive way
- **stunning** : extremely beautiful or attractive
- **identification** : an official document or other proof of one's identity
- **benevolent** : kind and helpful
- **compassionate** : showing feelings of sympathy for the suffering of others, often with a desire to help
- **conscientious** : putting a lot of effort into your work
- **easygoing** : relaxed and not easily upset or worried
- **extrovert** : characteristic of an extrovert
- **introvert** : characteristic of an introvert.
- **lofty** : behaving in a falsely superior or haughty manner
- **mischievous** : behaving or likely to behave in a naughty or troublesome way, but in fun and not meaning serious harm
- **stern** : severe, or showing disapproval
- **whole-hearted** : completely enthusiastic
- **withdrawn** : shy and quiet and preferring to be alone rather than with other people
- **executive education** : It is the term used for programs at graduate-level business schools that aim to give classes for Chief Executives and other top managers or entrepreneurs.

N.o.t.e

- **mentor** : a person who gives another person help and advice over a period of time and often also teaches them how to do their job
- **Certified Master Chef (C.M.C.)** : See appendix.
- **ACF** : See appendix.
- **bachelor' s degree** : a degree awarded on the successful completion of an undergraduate course at a college or university
- **master' s degree** : an academic degree higher than a bachelor's but lower than a doctor's
- **doctorate(=doctor' s degree)** : the highest degree from a university

R.e.f.e.r.n.c.e.s

http://bogglesworldesl.com/

http://dictionary.cambridge.org/

http://en.wikipedia.org/wiki/

http://encarta.msn.com/encnet/features/dictionary/

http://fpcctalkindian.nativeweb.org/nles3.htm

http://free-english-study.com/speaking/

http://starchefs.com/experts/chefs/

http://www.english-grammar-lessons.com/

http://www.englishgrammarsecrets.com/index.html

http://www.learn-english-today.com/free-english-lessons/

http://www.merriam-webster.com/

http://www.myenglishzone.com/

http://www.onelook.com/

Chapter 14 Level Three

1. Giving Opinions

1) Asking for Opinions

What do you think? What's your opinion? What are your ideas?
Do you have any thoughts on that? How do you feel about that?

2) Giving Opinions

I think they should leave for their internship.

I don't think we need a sous chef.

I believe (that) smoking should be outlawed in the kitchen.

I don't believe (that) kitchen work is a viable career choice.

In my opinion, your sliced onion is too thick but the slices are uniform, and that is more important.

I feel that it's the right thing to blanch the bones first.

I don't feel that my way is the only way to judge a good stock.

2. Asking for Details

1) Wh- Questions can be used to ask for more information:

Why is hollandaise considered a mother sauce?

How was his demo?

How do you make Kimchi from scratch?

What types of seafood are recommended for sushi, sashimi and why?

What type of mixing bowls do you recommend?

Where can I order wild mushrooms?

What is the best way to mark knives?

What is your most popular dish?

What is the proper side to serve a customer his meal, right or left?
Classically, dishes are placed from the left of the guest.

What annoys you in the kitchen?

What are the top schools in the Chicago area?

What is your specialty? Why?

What do you plan to do with the degree upon graduation?
How do you work as a team member and on your own?
What are the mental requirements to be a chef?

What is your prior experience with food and the foodservice industry?
What culinary literature are you reading?
What type of cuisine most interests you?
What are your long term culinary and non-culinary goals?

2) When asking for details about a particular item you are considering buying, you can say:

Could you give me some information about this recipe?

Can you give me more details about that dish washer?

Could you tell me about this kitchen fork?

What can you tell me about these kitchen scales?

3. Asking Permission

1) Modals are commonly used for asking permission.

Can I ask you a question? May I have a piece of cake?

Could I get you to turn off the oven?

2) Some other common phrases are:

Do you mind if I continue the tour of the kitchen?

Is it okay if I taste it?

Would you mind if I asked you "mental mise en place"?

Would it be all right if I borrowed your coffee machine?

3) Giving Permission

Sure. Go ahead. No problem.

4. Asking for and Giving Advice

1) Asking for Advice

What do you think I should do? What do you suggest?

What would you do (in this situation)?

2) Giving Advice

I think you should need to learn how to work with a woman on an equal level.

Maybe you should be able to identify the process of nouvelle cuisine.

Why don't you put the Bain-Marie on the pasta?

If I were you, I would take a continuing education course.

5. Sequencing

First, Second, Third, Last, First of all, Then, Next, Finally, To begin with,

Then, Later, In the end,

6. Discussing Sensitive Topics

1) Bringing up a sensitive topic

Can I talk to you for a minute? Can I ask you something?

Do you mind if I ask you something?   I need to talk to you for a minute.

I have to tell you something.   There's something I need to tell you.

There's something I think you should know.   We need to talk.

2) Prefacing a negative subject

I don't mean to be rude, but I suggest you hire an executive chef.

I hate to tell you this, but your onions are overcaramelized.

I don't know how to tell you this, but don't be afraid to challenge me on this stuff.

You might not like what I have to say, but you need to pick up the sense of urgency.

I wish I didn't have to tell you this, but again I want everybody to be clean.

This may be unpleasant, but if you can turn out one plate every two hours, you're never gonna get hired.

This may seem blunt, but regardless of background, everyone have to learn how to chop an onion.

7. Accepting and Refusing

1) Would you like some cake?

Yes, please.   Sure. Thanks   Okay. Thank you

No, thank you.   I'd better not.   No, but thanks for offering.

2) Would you like to catch Iron Chef on TV?

Okay. Sounds good. Sure. I'd love to. Yeah. Good idea

No, I'd rather not. I'm sorry, but I can't. No, but thanks for inviting me.

3) How about some more pie?

All right. Thanks Looks good. Thanks. Don't mind if I do.

No, thanks. I'm really full. Thanks anyway. Looks delicious, but I'll have to pass.

4) How about going shopping this weekend?

Great. What time? Sounds like fun. All right. When and where?

Sorry. I'm busy this weekend. I don't think I can. How about some other time?

8. Expressions for Descriptions

1) Sentences:

It is better to overcook than to undercook.

It is traditional in Korean restaurants for waiters to do the grilling.

The flames, the smoke, the dynamic action of the chef: this is something that Americans already like.

It's something that you create with a hot wok.

You can cook it up to 3 days in advance.

You can start with it.

You can use it to pierce a simmering carrot for tenderness, or to check whether a piece of braised lamb has softened.

It is used for chopping, slicing and even pounding and crushing (when you slam an ingredient with the side of the thick part of the blade).

You need it for making a toast.

You need/use it when you cut meat.

If you want/need to be profligate, then you can spend 6 euros on a steak.

2) Questions:

Is it grilled marinated beef?

What do you do with it? What is it made of?

What is it used for? What's the difference between A and B?

9. Indirect Requests and Information Exchange

1) Tell someone to do something

Please tell Helena to drain off the hot water from the pasta.

Could you tell Bob to call me?
Tell him not to do that.

2) Tell someone some information

Can you tell them (that) the dinner starts at nine?

Please tell Diana (that) I will be late.

3) Ask someone to do something

Please ask Tom to give me a call.

Could you ask Paula to be here at five?

4) Ask someone for some information (Yes or No)

Ask David if she is coming to the kitchen.

Could you ask them if they did the dishes?

Please ask her whether she finished slicing the whole tomato.

5) Ask someone for some information (Open ended)

Ask Paul what he is doing.

Please ask her when she will be here.

Would you ask him what he wants?

Will you ask them how much it costs?

N.o.t.e

-modal : a verb, such as 'can', 'might' and 'must', that is used with another verb to express an idea such as possibility that is not expressed by the main verb of a sentence

-nouvelle cuisine : a style of cooking in which food is lightly cooked and served in -attractive patterns on the plate in small amounts:

-Bain-Marie : a cooking utensil containing hot water into which another container is placed to keep food warm or cook it gently

R.e.f.e.r.n.c.e.s

http://bogglesworldesl.com/

http://dictionary.cambridge.org/

http://en.wikipedia.org/wiki/

http://encarta.msn.com/encnet/features/dictionary/

http://fpcctalkindian.nativeweb.org/nles3.htm

http://free-english-study.com/speaking/

http://starchefs.com/experts/chefs/

http://www.english-grammar-lessons.com/

http://www.englishgrammarsecrets.com/index.html

http://www.learn-english-today.com/free-english-lessons/

http://www.merriam-webster.com/

http://www.myenglishzone.com/

http://www.onelook.com/

Chapter 15 Level Four

1. Supporting Opinions

1) Giving your opinion

I think that the best way to eat healthfully is to concentrate on what you add to your diet, rather than what you try to leave out.

I don't think that most of them want to cook.

In my opinion, Korean chefs and Chinese chefs are much more skilled than French chefs.

2) Asking for support or details

Why do you think that? Could you elaborate? Could you give (me) an example?

Can you illustrate that? What evidence do you have?

Could you explain it in more detail? Could you provide some details?

3) Supporting your opinions

Let me illustrate, stock is the foundation for all classical French cooking.

For example, the Jews made their own wines because no kosher wines were available.

The flavor really only develops after multiple infusions. For instance, the same oolong leaf can normally be steeped six to eight times and often more.

To give you an example, Do you think you can learn to play golf by reading a book? Of course not.

Let me give you an example, for breakfast, I have 2 boiled eggs without the yolks.

To elaborate, I want these floors kept clean. If you see something on the floor, pick it up. I don't care if you didn't drop it. It's your floor; keep it clean.

First, the blend of grains from which the whiskey is distilled must be at least 51 percent corn. Second, the whiskey must be stored in charred new oak containers.

2. Exploring Options

1) Asking for input

Any ideas?　　What are the alternatives?

What do you think about a great stock which is usually judged by 5 criteria such as flavor, clarity, color, body, and aroma?

What do you think the Culinary Institute of America is called the most prominent cooking school in the world, a food-knowledge mecca?

How do you feel about the uniform policy?

How do you feel side towels are not for wiping your board?

2) Exploring Options

Let's look at Option 1. What (do you think) about Plan C?

How about the second alternative? Let's consider Randy's proposal.

3) Moving on

Let's move on to Option 3. What about Plan B?

Let's look at the third choice. How about Susan's idea?

Should we move on to the next point?

Before we move on, we need to consider contaminants when deciding which fish to eat.

3. Contrasting

On the other hand, I think the fat of lamb is an amazing flavor.

However, the company has focused less on ethnic dishes and more on sauces.

Yes, but my mother doesn't want me to cook, or my family doesn't want me to.

You may be right, but how do we quantify that?

I may be wrong, but I suspect that at least a few of these dark clouds have silver linings for consumers.

Correct me if I'm wrong, but I'm pretty sure that you make no mistake.

On the contrary, joy and laughter filled the kitchen.

4. Classifying

There are five kinds of thermometers that can help.

There are 85 types of sake on hand.

There are two categories of restaurant in Los Angeles. The first is a group of glitzy establishments serving fusion food of a sort known as California cuisine. The second camp, which makes Los Angeles a paradise for the adventurous diner, is made up of what are called, often with a patronizing wave, ethnic restaurants.

We can divide pizza dough into four equal parts, and then form each into a smooth ball.

The major for students is broken into seven sections. They are Korean Cuisine, Chinese Cuisine, Western Cuisine, Japanese Cuisine, Foodstyling, Beverage Innovation Management, and Foodservice Management.

5. Discussion Techniques

1) Opening a discussion

To begin with, you have to preheat the skillet or griddle, or the first batch will be nearly worthless.

We need to discuss(determine, find out) meat's freshness by looking at the date on its package, not at its color.

Let's start by raising the heat.

We'll start by hiring three line cooks.

The problem(issue, question) here is how much heat escapes without ever getting into the food.

The important thing (here) is to use excellent beef from a butcher.

The main thing we need to discuss is to get good chili powder and good cheese.

Let's look at the ingredient list here.

It looks like your potatoes are not cooked.

It appears that the era of the brasserie is over.

2) Asking for input

What do you think?

How about you?

How do you feel about that?

Any ideas on that?

3) Responding

(That sounds like a) good idea.

Sounds good.

The problem with that is that the chicken skin loses crispness as I add liquid to the pan to build the sauce.

That raises (brings up) the issue of why you would put perfectly good lobster meat in a pot pie.

6. Elaborating

1) Asking for Elaboration

Could you elaborate (on that)? Could you tell me a little more about it?

Could you give (me) some details? Could you fill me in on that?

Could you expound on that? What else can you tell us (about that)?

Is there anything else you can tell us? Is there more to it?

2) Elaborating

To elaborate, We have to eat more dark-green veggies like broccoli, spinach, and other dark leafy greens.

To give you more information, You have to stay within your daily calorie needs.

What's more, the researchers suggest that this early beverage was something different.

Let me explain. Let me elaborate.

Let me tell you a little more (about it).

Let me give you some details.

7. Clarifying

1) Clarifying your own ideas

In other words, I cooked it the way I would a custard.

What I mean is you can apply the same standards to your kitchen hygiene.

What I'm trying to say is I'm a person who love cooking.

What I wanted to say was I was the star of a wine panel tasting.

To clarify, he did not work on becoming a great chef.

2) Asking for Clarification

What do you mean (by that)? What are you trying to say?

What was that again? Could you clarify that?

3) Clarifying another's ideas

You mean the secret to great iced coffee is already in the kitchen.

What you mean is the coffee is grown in Colombia, Peru and Indonesia according to Fair Trade standards.

What you're saying is that we have to restart again.

(I think) what she means is the problem is solved.

What he's trying to say is he's real careful about what he cooks.

If I understand you, you're saying that you have to order overpriced drinks.

If I'm hearing you correctly, cheese, eggs and most other ingredients they have are organic.

So, you think (that) you can equip a real kitchen without much money.

So, your idea is kitchen equipment is purchased to make a dish easier to create.

8. Interrupting

1) Interrupting politely

Excuse me, Pardon me, Sorry to interrupt, May I interrupt (for a minute)?

Can I add something here? Could I inject something here?

Do you mind if I jump in here?

I don't mean to intrude, but I was wondering how important can 'eating well' be?

2) Getting back to the topic

Now, where was I? Where were we? What were you saying?

Anyway, I'm genuinely glad about the progress being made in the culinary world.

You were saying that vitamins are expensive urine.

To get back to better kitchen design.

9. Giving Instructions

1) Asking for Instructions

How do you obtain this texture?

How do I store greens?

What is the best way to keep pasta from getting sticky?

How do I go about it?

What do you suggest?

How do you suggest I proceed? I suggest that you believe "the customer is always right."

What is the first step? The first step is to warn people who may be late for the class.

2) Giving Instructions

① Sequencing

First, you look. Then, you taste. Next, you correct. Lastly, you enjoy.

② Starting out

Before you begin, you should melt butter in the same pan until it bubbles.

The first thing you do is to cut each in half and remove seed.

I would start by dissolve gelatin in the liquid.

The best place to begin is with butter, if you've never cooked with anchovies,

To begin with, heat the water to 185 degrees.

③ Continuing

After that, dip in egg mixture so that entire pepper is covered.

The next step is to season with spices and salt.

The next thing you do is turn the heat down to around 250.

Once you've done that, then remove with a slotted spoon and set aside.

When you finish that, then divide them into quarters.

④ Finishing

The last step is we should have a debate about French paradox.

The last thing you do is to have a correct dinner with wine.

In the end, he'll eat something green.

When you've finished, there is time to grill some vegetables.

When you've completed all the steps, taste and adjust seasoning if necessary.

10. Simple Presentations

1) Introduction

(Good morning, afternoon, evening) I'm happy to be here.

I'm glad to have this opportunity to have a good wine.

Today, I'd like to talk (to you) about wine tasting.

My topic today is making a great stock.

The focus of my remarks is learning the basics.

I'd like to share some thoughts on food, cooking and eating.

2) Main points

Let me start by knowing how to dig information.

First, let me tell you about tonight's specials.

I've divided my topic into (three) parts: (They are beginner's level, intermediate level, and advanced level)

3) Giving examples

For instance, you learn how to cook using your real kitchen, not a fantasy one.

Let me illustrate, what I have in mind.

To illustrate, he picked samples of four important varieties.

4) Conclusion

In conclusion, we would like simply to offer the three following remarks.

To conclude, the results would be soup, not sauce.

To summarize, you can find a lot of information on how to get rich quick.

To sum up, this is the renamed Korean restaurant with prominent kitchens.

11. Checking for Understanding

1) Checking for Understanding

(Do you) know what I mean? Do you know what I'm saying?

Do you understand? Are you following me? Are you with me (so far)?

Have you got it? Any questions? Got it?

2) Showing Understanding

I see. / I understand. / I get it.(I got it) / Gotcha.(Informal)

3) Expressing Lack of Understanding

I don'get it. (I'm sorry.) I don't understand. What do you mean?

I'm not following you. I don't quite follow you. What was that again?

I'm not sure I get what you mean.

12. Conceding to Make a Point

That may be true, but nothing has been proved.

I may be wrong, but you need something salty.

You might be right, but all the dishes make us feel healthy.

You have a good point, but you are missing the point.

You could say that, but french wines are still the best values.

Correct me if I'm wrong, but yogurt is "a cow" milk product which babies should not consume until after one year old.

I don't mean to be rude, but I don't know what's going in your kitchen.

I hate to bring this up, but we're running short of money.

I don't mean to be negative, but wine adds another dimension to the meal.

This may sound strange, but it's genuine.

13. Analyzing Problems

1) Focusing on the main problem/issue

What is the main problem? What is the real issue (here)?

(I think) the major problem is the technique works only if the skin is perfectly intact.

Our primary concern is the safety of all our employees.

The crux of the matter is maintaining quality.

(As I see it), the most important thing is that oysters have to be fresh.

The main problem we need to solve is that the menu has to be simplified and divided into appetizers, main courses and desserts.

We really need to take care of the animals because they take care of us.

It all comes down to this : Keep the customer comfortable.

2) Asking for input

What should we do about it? What needs to be done?

What do you think we should do? What are we going to do about it?

Do you have any suggestions?   Any ideas?

3) Making Recommendations

I recommend that you work the first shift in the morning.

I suggest that every restaurant and store manager sit in a manual wheelchair and personally experience how disabled guests actually experience their establishment.

I would like to propose that you start cooking pasta in a way that your instructor chef taught you.

Why don't we try something hot?

N.o.t.e

- **leave out** : to fail to include somebody or something, whether by choice or accident
- **elaborate** : to add more information to or explain something that you have said
- **jew** : a member of a race of people whose traditional religion is Judaism
- **kosher** : (of food or places where food is sold etc.) prepared or kept in conditions that follow the rules of Jewish law
- **infusion** : when one thing is added to another to make it stronger or better
- **steep** : to cause to stay in a liquid, especially in order to become soft or clean or to improve flavour
- **charred** : burnt and black

N.o.t.e

–**clarity** : the quality of being clear, pure, or transparent

–**glitzy** : having a fashionable appearance intended to attract attention

–**sort of** : a group of things which are of the same type or which share similar qualities, 원래는 sort of 가 명사 앞에 놓여 쓰이지만(We both like the same sort of music.) 본문과 같이 명사 뒤에 of sort를 놓고 쓰는 경우도 있음.(I'm going to have a salad of some sort.)

–**patronizing** : displaying or indicative of an offensively condes -cending manner

–**wave** : an unusually large number of events of a similar, often bad, type, happening within the same period

–**brasserie** : a French-style restaurant that serves cheap and simple food

–**fill *sb* in** (GIVE INFORMATION) : to give someone extra or missing information

–**expound** : to give a detailed explanation of something

–**inject** : to introduce something new that is necessary or helpful to a situation or process

–**jump in** : to interrupt when someone else is speaking

–**intrude** : to go into a place or situation in which you are not wanted or not expected to be

–**concede** : to allow someone to have something, even though you do not want to

–**crux** : the most important or serious part of a matter, problem or argument

–**come down to** : to mean or represent something fundamentally, when all nonessential detail has been disregarded

R.e.f.e.r.n.c.e.s

http://bogglesworldesl.com/

http://dictionary.cambridge.org/

http://en.wikipedia.org/wiki/

http://encarta.msn.com/encnet/features/dictionary/

http://fpcctalkindian.nativeweb.org/nles3.htm

http://free-english-study.com/speaking/

http://starchefs.com/experts/chefs/

http://www.english-grammar-lessons.com/

http://www.englishgrammarsecrets.com/index.html

http://www.learn-english-today.com/free-english-lessons/

http://www.merriam-webster.com/

http://www.myenglishzone.com/

http://www.onelook.com/

Chapter 16 Level Five

1. Commenting Phrases for Conversation

1) If you would like to make a comment or insert a remark in an ongoing conversation, it is polite to acknowledge what someone has just said before stating your own ideas. Here are some phrases.

That's interesting. I think that cooking is a very sexy thing.

Interesting point. I would add one more: how long should I work overtime?

Hmmm. I hadn't thought of that before.

2) Questions can also be a useful way of bringing new ideas into a conversation:

What do you think about a true chef?

Have you considered eating spoonworms?

What about the rest of the menu?

3) Sometimes a more direct approach is appropriate:

Can I add something here?

(Do you) mind if I interject something here?

2. Paraphrasing Phrases for Conversation

so . . . (rephrase the other person's ideas)

Its 16 stools are perpetually occupied, so you will probably have to eat on your feet.

In other words . . . (paraphrase)

The draft document also further reduces salt intake and specifically recommends low-fat milk and fish heavy in omega-3 fatty acids. It limits alcoholic drinks to one (women) or two (men) a day. The proposed guidelines also for the first time emphasize exercise, suggesting 30 to 90 minutes a day. In other words, eat better and exercise more.

I understand. You're saying that Escoffier was a great french chef?

Oh. I see. You want to say that this is good for our health.

I get it. You mean we can increase the amount if we like.

So, What you mean is not what I said.

Let me see if I understand you correctly; do you mean one or two?

What I think you're saying is "Nobody is being forced to buy this food."

If I'm hearing you correctly, are you saying that reservations are a must?

N.o.t.e

–stool : a seat without any support for the back or arms

R.e.f.e.r.n.c.e.s

http://bogglesworldesl.com/

http://dictionary.cambridge.org/

http://encarta.msn.com/encnet/features/dictionary/

http://fpcctalkindian.nativeweb.org/nles3.htm

http://free-english-study.com/speaking/

http://www.english-grammar-lessons.com/

http://www.englishgrammarsecrets.com/index.html

http://www.learn-english-today.com/free-english-lessons/

http://www.myenglishzone.com/

Guide to Kitchen Enlgish

Part Ⅳ

Employment and Success

Guide to Kitchen English

Chapter 17 Examples of Career Opportunities

1. Career Opportunity for a Foodservice Company

This is an example of a career opportunity for a position of Korean Chef. Let's look at its skills and qualifications a Foodservice Company requires.

Skills and Qualifications:

- Certificate in Korean and Japanese Culinary Arts
- Two (2) to three (3) years of culinary experience in Korean and Japanese cuisine within a food service operation
- Minimum of two (2) to three (3) years of culinary/kitchen supervision experience
- Knowledge of Korean food trends with a focus on quality, production, sanitation, food cost controls, and presentation
- Experience in planning and producing from a culinary perspective
- Batch cooking or high volume cooking experience preferred
- Food production experience for large catering or banquet functions
- ServSafe® or equivalent Certified
- Knowledge of diet principles as well as safe and sanitary food handling principles

- Understanding of financial, budgetary, and food control practices
- Good supervisory, leadership, management and coaching skills
- Excellent communication skills in Korean and basic English to understand and follow recipe
- Ability to communicate on various levels including management, departmental, customer and associate levels

2. Career Opportunity for a Restaurant Group

Here is an another example of a career opportunity for a position of Kitchen Manager. Let's look at its job requirements a Restaurant Group presents.

Job requirements :

- Responsible for all kitchen operational duties.
- Weekly schedule for all kitchen sections.
- Responsible for the daily ordering and receiving issues
- Responsible of the weekly and monthly inventory.
- Food cost Analysis
- Ensure the recipe execution.
- To communicate with the purchasing department regarding the consistency of the agreed brand quality and to participate in evaluating any alternative product.
- Forecast the yearly and quarterly product consumption.
- To communicate with the Kitchen chef regarding all the kitchen related issues.
- To supervise the commissary staff and to ensure the hygiene and sanitation execution.

- Able to monitor 52 kitchen staff.

Skills:

- Computer literate
- Good command of English and Arabic

Education:

Hotel Management or any equivalent degree

N.o.t.e

–**Batch** : a group of things or people dealt with at the same time or considered similar in type

–**ServSafe®** : It is a nationally recognized food safety training and certification program established by the National Restaurant Association.

–**issue** : supplies (as food or clothing or ammunition) issued by the government

–**commissary** : a shop which supplies food and goods, especially to people in the army or in prison

–**literate** : having knowledge of a particular subject, or a particular type of knowledge

R.e.f.e.r.n.c.e.s

http://www.bbc.co.uk/food/glossary/

http://regionalhelpwanted.com/

http://www.bayt.com/job/

Chapter 18 Preparing for a Job Interview

This chapter explores some of the questions most job interviews contain, and something important interviewees consider in advance. Let's look at them!

1. Job interview questions interviewees hear

In a nutshell, a job interview is a question and answer session. Most job interviews contain at least a few similar questions, including some variation of the following:

- Tell me about yourself.
- Tell me about your background, accomplishments, strengths and weaknesses.
- Where do you see yourself in five years?
- What was most/least rewarding about college (or your last job)?
- How do you measure personal success?
- How would you describe your most recent job performance?
- Why did you choose to apply for this job (or this company)?
- What are your strengths/weaknesses?
- What motivates you?
- What interests you about our company?
- Describe a situation in which you had to deal with a difficult person.

How did you handle the situation?

- Why did you select your college (or course of study)?
- How do you work under pressure?
- How would you handle a situation in which meeting a deadline was impossible?
- How can you contribute to this organization?
- How would a friend (or former colleague or professor) describe you?
- Describe a situation in which you disagreed with your supervisor. How did you handle it?
- Do you work well on a team?
- Who was your most difficult boss and why?
- What outside activities are most significant to your personal development?
- Where do you see yourself in five years? In ten years?

2. Some things interviewees consider in advance

Expect to hear something like some of the questions above. But memorizing good answers is just the first step for preparing for a job interview. Consider some of the following.

1) Do your research

A little information about a company will let you demonstrate your knowledge (and interest) during the interview. Spend a few hours becoming familiar with the company, its products or services, the industry in which it operates, and how your skills will contribute to the organization. Then, when a recruiter asks why you want to work for their company, you'll have enough knowledge to form an impressive answer. Things you should research include the age and size of the company, the customers, the major competitors, its industry reputation, the location of corporate headquarters, the backgrounds of the managers, advancement opportunities, and if there have been recent layoffs. If you can't find answers to some of your questions about a company, ask during the interview.

2) Secure your references

Pick at least three people (former supervisors, colleagues, professors, a parent of a friend who've known you since childhood) who are willing to be your references. Be sure to ask their permission to be listed as a reference beforehand, and—of course!—be certain that they will speak well of you if a potential employer contacts them.

3) Know where you're going

Find out exactly how to get to the interview site. If you've never been there before, think about taking a trial drive to the location a few days before the interview (and even then, give yourself more time in case you run into traffic). If your car's like your second living room, get it washed and cleaned on the inside. You never know who might see you in the parking lot-maybe even the person interviewing you.

4) Arrive early

Get to the interview site at least 15 minutes before the interview. Visit the restroom and check your appearance. Announce yourself to the receptionist to let him or her know that you have arrived for an appointment. Turn your cell phone off so it doesn't ring during your meeting.

5) Bring the right documentation

Make a checklist of things you will need for the interview and make sure you have them in your briefcase before leaving home. You should have extra copies of your resume; a portfolio, writing samples, or other professional work; letters of reference; your college transcripts (if you're a recent graduate); and proof of who you are, like a passport, Social Security card, or driver's license. You should also carry a pen and paper for taking notes, and suitable reading material in case you have to wait in the reception area.

6) Battling your nerves

It's only natural to be a little nervous before a job interview—and a little extra adrenaline helps you do you best! But you have to find a way to keep the adrenaline, and your nerves, under control.

Here are a few things to keep in mind :

① Be organized : Listen to the weather forecast (and if it might rain, find your umbrella) Make sure you have enough gas in your car. Double-check to make sure your suit is clean and pressed, and that your briefcase is fully loaded. Find out whom you should call if, for some reason, you run into a problem.

② Get a good night's sleep the night before. Lay off the spicy or rich foods and alcohol on the evening before the big day and be well-hydrated.

③ Stick to your routine. On the day of your interview, try to do things as you normally would. Wake up at your normal time (or a few minutes earlier). Eat what you normally eat. And if you're a coffee drinker, this is not the day to try decaffeinating yourself!

④ Pay attention to your breathing. When you're nervous, your breathing becomes more shallow, which only adds to the anxiety you're feeling.

Think about your breathing, and as soon as you feel the slightest sense that your breathing is becoming more rapid than normal, focus on taking deeper, slower breaths.

⑤ Remember to smile. Keep smiling, from the minute you walk into the interview site. It's a job interview, not a courtroom sentencing. Try to have a good time. If a receptionist strikes up a conversation, keep it going. Make eye contact. Just be yourself. And smile.

7) Here are some questions you might ask.

- What would I be expected to accomplish in this position?
- What are the greatest challenges in this position?
- How do you think I fit the position?

N.o.t.e

- **In a nutshell** : as few words as possible
- **rewarding** : giving a reward, especially by making you feel satisfied that you have done something important or useful, or done something well
- **layoffs** : The act of suspending or dismissing an employee, as for lack of work or because of corporate reorganization.
- **reference** : a written statement describing your character and abilities, esp. when you are trying to get a new job, or the person who writes this statement
- **run into *obj* (MEET)** : to meet (someone) by chance, or to experience (esp. something unpleasant) unexpectedly
- **adrenaline** : a hormone (= chemical substance) produced by the body when a person is frightened, angry, or excited, which makes the heart beat faster and prepares the body to react to danger
- **Lay off(Informal)** : to cease or quit
- **shallow breathing** : breathing in which you only take a small amount of air into your lungs with each breath
- **courtroom** : a room where a court of law meets
- **strike up *sth* (RELATE)** : to start a relationship or conversation with someone

R.e.f.e.r.n.c.e.s

http://www.cliffsnotes.com/

http://www.roberthalffinance.com/

http://dictionary.cambridge.org/

http://encarta.msn.com/encnet/features/dictionary/

http://www.merriam-webster.com/

http://www.onelook.com/

Chapter 19 Job Interview Question and Answer English Tips

Congratulations! You have applied for a job and now you are getting ready for that important job interview. Your English is excellent and you are looking forward to making a good impression on your future (hopefully) boss. Now, you need to make sure that you also have the right type of English for that job interview.

The job interview in English contains specific questions and appropriate answers. It also requires a certain flexibility in your usage of tenses. This feature provides tips on job interview questions and answers in English.

When you walk in the room the very first impression you make on the interviewer can have a great influence on the rest of the interview. It is important that you introduce yourself, shake hands, and are friendly. The first question is often a "breaking the ice" (establish a rapport) type of question. Don't be surprised if the interviewer asks you something like:

- How are you today?
- Did you have any trouble finding us?
- What do you think of the weather lately?

Don't be surprised by the friendly tone. The interviewer wants to put you at ease (help you relax). Answer the question without going into too much detail. The language you use should be simple but polite, for example;

How are you today?

GOOD

I'm fine thank you, and you?

I'm well thank you.

BAD

So, so

OK

Not so well

1. What is most important?

Talking about your experience and credentials (qualifications) is the most important part of any job interview. Your qualifications include your education from High School on and any special training you may have done in the past. Your experience is any work that you have done that is directly or indirectly related to the job you are applying for.

1) Education

Remember that your education took place in the past. Therefore you need to use the past tenses, for example:

I attended Hyejeon College from 1997 to 2003.

I graduated with an associate in Culinary Arts.

Etc.

If you are currently a student you should use the following present tenses :

I am currently studying at the University of New York and will graduate with a degree in Economics in the spring.

I am studying English at the Borough Community College.

Etc.

Remember to include any training you may have had when talking about your education. This includes any computer training, correspondence courses, etc. Make sure to mention your English studies. This is very important as English is not your first language and the employer may be concerned about this fact. Assure the employer that you are continuing to improve your English skills by any courses you may be taking, or by saying that you study a certain number of hours a week to improve your skills.

2) Experience and Qualifications

Work experience is by far the most important topic of any job interview (at least in the United States and Britain). Therefore, it is important to explain what experience you have in detail. Generally, employers want to know exactly what you did and how well you accomplished your tasks. This is not the time to be modest. Be confident, and talk freely about your accomplishments in past employment.

The tenses you should use are the following:

When talking about current employment be careful to use the present perfect or present perfect continuous. This signals that you are still performing these tasks at your current job, for example:

Smith and Co. have employed me for the last 3 years as a salesperson.

I have been creating customer contacts for 6 months.

Etc.

When talking about past employers use the past tenses to signal that you are no longer working for that company, for example:

I was employed by Jackson's from 1996 to 1998 as a clerk.

I worked as a receptionist at the Ritz while I was living in New York.

Etc.

2. Talking about Responsibilities

Most importantly, you will need to demonstrate your qualifications and skills, which are required for the job you are applying for. The job skills that you have acquired in the past may not have been for the same exact job. Therefore, it is important to show how the capabilities you do have relate to the job you are applying for.

I remember a wonderful example of adapting skills to fit the job desired. I had a student from Moscow who had worked as the manager of an important theater in Moscow. Unfortunately, he had to start from the beginning in New York and therefore wanted to get a job as a rodent exterminator (someone who kills rats!). When asked what kind of experience he had, he replied that, as the manager of the theater, he had had to make sure that the theater was always rodent free and was therefore capable of doing the job well! This is a fantastic example of the type of adaptability most employers in the United States are looking for.

1) Use the Right Word

Below is a list of great verbs to help you express just exactly what you did with impressive vocabulary. These verbs are used to express responsibilities and tasks performed:

acted, accomplished, adapted, administered, advanced, advised, allocated, analyzed, applied, approved, arbitrated, arranged, assisted, attained, blended, brought, built, carried out, catalogued, changed, classified, collaborated, compared, completed, computed, conceived, conducted, constructed, consulted, contracted, controlled, cooperated, coordinated, corrected, counseled, created, dealt, decided, decreased, defined, delegated, derived, designated, detected, developed, devised, directed, discovered, distributed, documented, doubled, edited, encouraged, engineered, enlarged, escalated, established, estimated, evaluated, examined, expanded, experienced, explored, facilitated, finalized, formulated, founded, functioned, governed, grouped, guided, handled, harmonized, harnessed, headed, identified, implemented, improved, increased, indexed, initiated, inspected, installed, instituted, interpreted, introduced, invented, investigated, justified, led, localized, located, made, managed, maintained, mechanized, merged, moderated, motivated, negotiated, opened, operated, organized, originated, overcame, perceived, performed, pioneered, planned, prepared, presented, presided, processed, programmed, promoted, provided, purchased, raised, recommended, recorded, recruited, rectified, redesigned, repaired, replaced, restored, reversed, reviewed, revised, saved, screened, selected, serviced, set up, solved, sorted, sparked, specified, started, stimulated, strengthened, summarized, supervised, supported, systematized, tested, trained, transacted, transcribed, transformed, tripled, upgraded, validated, varied, verified, vitalized, won, wrote

2) To describe your skills the following adjectives are useful

accurate, active, adaptable, adept, broad-minded, competent, conscientious, creative, dependable, determined, diplomatic, discreet, efficient, energetic, enterprising, enthusiastic, experienced, fair, firm, genuine, honest, innovative, logical, loyal, mature, methodical, motivated, objective, outgoing, personable, pleasant, positive, practical, productive, reliable, resourceful, self-disciplined, sense of humor, sensitive, sincere, successful, tactful, trustworthy

Use these verbs and adjectives and really sell yourself. You only have a few minutes to show how good you really are. By using this precise vocabulary and being confident can help you make the best impression possible.

N.o.t.e

- **rapport** : a good understanding of someone and an ability to communicate well with them
- **credentials** : the abilities and experience which make someone suitable for a particular job or activity, or proof of someone's abilities and experience
- **rodent** : any of various small mammals with large sharp front teeth, such as mice and rats
- **exterminate** : to kill all the animals or people in a particular place or of a particular type
- **arbitrate** : to make a judgment in an argument, usually because asked to do so by those involved
- **catalogue** : to record something, especially in a list

N.o.t.e

- **collaborate** : to work with someone else for a special purpose
- **delegate** : to give a particular job, duty, right, etc. to someone else so that they do it for you
- **derive *sth* from *sth*** : to get or obtain something from something else
- **designate** : to choose someone officially to do a particular job
- **engineer** : to arrange cleverly and often secretly for something to happen, especially something that is to your advantage
- **harness** : to control something, usually in order to use its power
- **index** : to vary a system of numbers against each other or against a fixed standard
- **pioneer** : to experiment with or develop something new
- **preside** : to be in charge of a formal meeting or ceremony
- **rectify** : to correct something or make something right
- **reverse** : to (cause something to) go backwards, or to change the direction, order, position, result, etc. of something to its opposite
- **screen** : to protect someone by taking the blame yourself
- **spark** : to cause the start of something, especially an argument or fighting
- **specify** : to state or describe something clearly and exactly
- **transact** : to do and complete a business activity
- **transcribe** : to record something written, spoken or played by writing it down
- **validate** : to make something officially acceptable or approved, especially after examining it
- **verify** : to prove that something exists or is true, or to make certain that something is correct

N.o.t.e

- **vitalize** : to make somebody or something lively
  -adaptable : able or willing to change in order to suit different conditions
- **adept** : having a natural ability to do something that needs skill
- **competent** : able to do something well
- **discreet** : careful not to cause embarrassment or attract too much attention, especially by keeping something secret
- **enterprising** : good at thinking of and doing new and difficult things, especially things that will make money
- **methodical** : describes people who do things in a very ordered, careful way
- **resourceful** : skilled at solving problems and making decisions on your own
- **self-disciplined** : capable of or subject to self-discipline
- **tactful** : careful not to say or do anything that could upset someone
- **trustworthy** : able to be trusted

R.e.f.e.r.n.c.e.s

http://www.roberthalffinance.com/

http://esl.about.com/library/weekly/aa113097.htm

http://dictionary.cambridge.org/

http://encarta.msn.com/encnet/features/dictionary/

http://www.merriam-webster.com/

http://www.onelook.com/

Chapter 20 Examples for Lifelong Student and Continuing Education

The following stories are success stories about chefs who participated in ProChef program by CIA, which gives non-commercial chefs the chance to prove and improve their cooking and management skills.

1. ProChef Level II Success Story; Judy Doherty

After graduating from CIA in 1982, I became a pastry chef. I have 15 years of strong industry experience, including 10 years as Executive Pastry Chef for Hyatt hotels. Ten years ago, I began my own company, Food and Health Communications, researching and developing healthy recipes and cooking methods.

Recently, I was visiting the CIA website. I am not sure why; maybe to find a picture of the school to show a friend. But I will never forget my reaction when I stumbled upon their ProChef Certification program. My reaction was nothing short of, "I want that!"

And so my ProChef journey at CIA began.

Since graduation from CIA and my work experience gave me ProChef Level I status, I was able to resume my studies at Level II. From the start, I was optimistic; of the four major culinary competencies listed, I already had two in my pocket: baking/pastry and healthy cooking. I was delighted to see that ProChef II required a command of Mediterranean cooking. Honestly, returning to school had begun as a fun idea. I felt that listing ProChef Level II certification on my FoodAndHealth.com website would be impressive. But now I realized that learning Mediterranean cooking methods would benefit my business.

So I printed out the study guide and bought some books and videos on the CIA list. I signed up for the Mediterranean Cuisine: Ingredients and Techniques class and then picked a date to take the test in December of 2005.

I found a great resource in David Edens, a California-based chef who took the ProChef II exam. He gave me many helpful tips. But he also gave me a wake-up call: ProChef II involves taking 11 tests over four days. It sounded pretty tough. However, I learned that ProChef II is a stepping stone to the Certified Master Chef test.

Two weeks before the ProChef II test, I was cooking every day to practice. I made pâté and fabricated meat and fish. I practiced making many dishes in Mediterranean cuisine style, and brushed up on aspects of baking, healthy cooking and garde manger.

While I was at the CIA for the Mediterranean cooking class, I made good use of my time. Before each class, I studied the history and culture of the Mediterranean region. The Mediterranean class was taught by a Certified Master Chef Ken Arnone. I really enjoyed making and eating dishes. I also visited the library and ate at all the restaurants on campus, especially the Caterina de' Medici.

Since I enjoyed the Mediterranean class so much, I signed up for the Charcuterie, Smokehouse and Condiment Workshop. Charcuterie proved to be a great decision. Now I was really working hard on my study guide. I talked to many instructors and was surprised at how readily they were willing to share information and tips.

Test week was challenging. The mornings were packed with taking tests, preparing garde manger food items and making menus and prep lists. The evenings were spent on cooking exams, which didn't get us out of class until 7 or 8 p.m.

The first day was baking. I figured it would feel nice to "come out of the gate" on familiar ground. But even that test was challenging for a veteran baker like me. Why? First, you're in a different kitchen from your own with different equipment, ingredients and conditions. Second, you have people watching you. You have to work quickly, neatly and efficiently. You have to serve everything on time. And finally, you have to discuss your day's performance: why and how you made your dishes and what you would do differently the next time.

At the end of each day, I would learn if I passed and was still in the running. I would be relieved. But I also worried about the next day.

By the last day of ProChef II, however, I came to really appreciate this experience. The chefs cared so much about helping us. They went above and beyond to share their knowledge. They emphasized flavor and purpose and the craft of the kitchen that makes us chefs.

Our moderating chef told us on the first day that the ProChef II experience would make us much better chefs. He was right.

Honestly, I went into this ProChef Level II certification looking to get a snazzy little plug on my website, I got so much more. It really wasn't about the destination; it was about the journey. I acquired a much greater awareness for my cooking. Definitely a finer skill level. The CIA chef instructors treated us all as if we were all future candidates for the Certified Master Chef exam. We even had a guest master chef address the class. He had so much wisdom and insight on how to make food taste good and look good and just make sense. He gave us a critique as though we were taking his test. I learned so much and am grateful for that.

I have a whole new set of goals for myself. I want to travel in the Mediterranean and learn even more about that food. I want to visit the spice market of Istanbul. I will concentrate more on making my knife cuts more perfect instead of just going through the motions to get that done. My cooking will have a whole new life and I really love my trade all over again.

I want to go back to the CIA every year for continuing education. And of course I want to take the ProChef Level III course. I am already researching that now so I can fit the Asian, Latin and wine classes into my schedule—and my bags are not even unpacked.

N.o.t.e

- **stumble across/on/upon *sth/sb***: to discover something by chance, or to meet someone by chance
- **be nothing short of** : used to emphasize a bad situation, quality or type of behaviour
- **brush up on *sth***: to improve your knowledge of something already learned but partly forgotten
- **Charcuterie** : a delicatessen that specializes in meats
- **moderating** : lessening in intensity or strength
- **snazzy** : modern and stylish in a way that attracts attention
- **critique** : a report of something such as a political situation or system or a person's work or ideas, which examines it and provides an often negative judgment

2. ProChef Level III Success Story; Executive Chef, Steve Hickman, C.E.C.

Steve Hickman knows what it means to work hard. From humble beginnings as a dishwasher to executive chef of the Hillsdale Community Health Center in Hillsdale, MI, his 20 years in the business has been a challenging and rewarding venture. "I never received formal training in the culinary arts, so I had to work from the bottom up", he said. "My training came from working in private restaurants, a major hotel chain, and country clubs."

Today, Steve looks to the professionals at The Culinary Institute of America for continuing education. "It wasn't hard for me to decide what school to attend for professional development," he said. "I wanted to come to the top school in the country, and for me that meant the CIA. I've learned a lot from the chef-instructors because they are very flexible, and with each new course they share different views and expertise."

Since 2004, Steve has participated in more than 20 professional development courses at the CIA. Like many experienced chefs, he knows that staying current in the industry is essential to his success. "At the CIA, I've had the opportunity to experiment with other cuisines, fine-tune my skills, attain a solid level of confidence, and meet people from all over the world in every facet of the industry," he said. "Professional development courses have definitely been beneficial to my career."

Steve's professional development at the CIA has extended beyond continuing education courses. In May 2005, he received ProChef Level III Certification and earned the title of Certified Executive Chef from the American Culinary Federation (ACF). "Going through the levels was a challenge, but I was prepared and felt confident because of the courses I had taken prior to the exams."

"ProChef Certification gave me immediate recognition among my peers, the CIA, and the ACF," he said. "My employer is satisfied with my achievement, my customers have increased respect for my work, and I've learned more than I ever thought I would."

N.o.t.e

- **C.E.C.** : the title of Certified Executive Chef from the American Culinary Federation (ACF)
- **fine-tune** : to make very small changes to something in order to make it work as well as possible

3. ProChef Level III Success Story ; Chef Patrick Wilson

In 1979, I was a student at The Culinary Institute of America. One day, my instructor Craig Goldstein, gave our class advice I will always remember: We should continue training as chefs for our whole careers. I raised my hand to ask why, and he explained, “Patrick, the next generation of culinary students will be computer literate and bi-lingual by the time they are out of high school. They may be able to do your job quicker, faster and for less money than a lot of you, unless you continue to upgrade, learn and improve your whole careers.”

I heeded Craig Goldstein. That's why my career continues to grow. That's why I am currently deploying onboard the Navy ship USS Baatan, working with the galley crew and chefs. In this new technological world, 27 years of cooking experience alone are not enough. You have to keep up with modern equipment. So, when a sailor asks for a recipe or requires a PowerPoint presentation, I have the goods on my laptop computer.

The value of ongoing education has surfaced often in my career. In 2001, I interviewed at The Saint Andrew's Golf Club. Located in Hastings-on-Hudson, New York, this is America's oldest golf club. There were 250 applicants for the position. I made it to the third interview. Club president Mr. Michael Beckerich asked me, “Are you a Certified Executive Chef (CEC) with the American Culinary Federation (ACF).” I sat silently and Mr. Goldstein's words rushed back. Without ongoing education, I would become obsolete in this fast-changing industry.

Luckily, I got the job. But I began to do research. How do I upgrade my skills, to improve my impact and then provide the best food for the

Saint Andrew's membership? After all, many club members live in Manhattan, which offers the best cuisine in the world. To get them to stay for dinner after golf, I would have to offer a dining experience and menu of highest quality. To be able to offer the best meant staying on top of food trends and other aspects of maintaining a restaurant and kitchen.

I have made sure that the Saint Andrew's food calendar offers numerous theme nights which highlight cuisines from around the world. That's why I read about the newest foods and trends in eating. That's why I also returned to CIA for the ProChef certification program. The Saint Andrew's Golf Club board of directors supports my ongoing training. They have been financially supportive, and allow me time off to compete in American Culinary Federation events.

The ProChef Certification Program is about learning and growing. I took Level I for the chance to cover basic cooking methods. On the first day of Level I, I had to make a French Omelet. That seemed easy, considering I entered the industry as a breakfast chef at a Catkills resort. But I received a poor grade in egg cookery. My omelet was not up to the baseline expectation as outlined in the ProChef Level I study guide. The kitchen proctors, Chefs Hinnerk Von Bargen and David Kamen, encouraged me to keep trying until I perfected it. Eventually, I did. After my poor performance on the first day, I committed myself to staying on task and to perform above the baseline. Those efforts were rewarded with significantly improved grades. Level I covered culinary math, food costing, egg cookery, food safety, nutrition, product identification, cooking methods, soups, stocks and culinary fundamentals.

In preparation for the Level II exam, The Culinary Institute of America offers various classes. I enrolled in three to complement my abilities: Charcuterie, Smokehouse &Condiment Workshop, Techniques of Healthy Cooking and Mediterranean Cuisine: Ingredients and Techniques. These classes were immensely beneficial to my cooking skills and prepared me for the Pro Chef Level II exam.

After completing Pro Chef Level II, I took my newfound talents on the road in March of 2005. In Columbus, OH, I entered an ACF-sanctioned competition and tested my skills in fish, poultry and hot- and cold-plated desserts. I earned my first silver medal in cold plated pastry and three bronze medals.

Level III was a long and rewarding journey; I began studies immediately after Level II and worked in some ethnic restaurants, learning new techniques in Asian and Indian fare. I also dined in many Latin, Caribbean and Mexican restaurants, trying to understand the use of ingredients. My friend, Chef Richard Yoshida of House of Yoshida in Bethel, CT, trained me in Sushi, Sashimi, Udon noodles, different Dashi and stocks. Chef Yoshida put me to work right behind the counter with the other highly trained sushi &sashimi chefs for on the job training. I asked Chef Yoshida for guidance in purchasing equipment to make Sushi and Sashimi. Richard selected a cedar bowl to mix the rice, a special knife made in Japan and a fan to cool the sushi rice. Learning the proper technique of rice and the sushi rice preparation is part of the journey. My time spent in an Indian restaurant near my home was equally rewarding. Chef Pramod Menon of Kolam Restaurant in Newtown, CT, was enthusiastic about allowing my presence in his kitchen. Chef Menon taught me how to make assorted Dosas, Vindaloo, Naam, Chutneys, Curries as well as the use of spices. Each night after the different stages in the restaurants, I would order a large variety of dishes to go and get the chance to watch the preparation. One Stage in a Korean Restaurant was total entertainment.

My Korean is very weak and the Korean Chef's English was equally weak. The communication was accomplished with visual and animated gestures, sounds and the actual cooking of foods. The Korean chefs would offering encouraging words with their limited English, by saying 'look over here', 'over there', 'watch me', 'try this'. I was laughing most of the time spent in the kitchen. The Korean chefs were surprised that someone would want to learn about their cooking methods and ingredients. Until now, preparing food for the Ladies Golf Association's events at Saint Andrew's have always been challenging. But learning Korean BBQ has enhanced my offerings to the club members and varied their dining experiences.

This accreditation program and exams are thorough, challenging and ultimately rewarding. I study new food trends as well as management skills and restaurant computer technology. The ProChef courses at CIA evaluate my cooking ability, but also my skills in maintaining a kitchen, staff and even keeping control of proper sanitation procedures.

This upcoming year looks to be a very exciting year at The Saint Andrew's Golf Club. I will offer a new variety of theme nights inspired by my research, learning and testing at The Culinary Institute of America's ProChef Certification Program. They include: Paella night, including complementary Spanish wines. A night of Sushi, Sashimi &Abalone. Bistro Fare night features items like Choux Croute, Cassolet, Duck Confit, Terrines and Pates. These theme nights join our traditional Lobster and New York Steak House Nights. The Board of Governors' support is motivating to reach new heights. I plan a new format for the menus. One side will offer "Club Fare," i.e. the comfort food some members crave. The "Other Side" will offer more progressive fare.

On our daily menu at Saint Andrew's, I serve simple quality fare like Pennsylvania Roast Organic Chickens with Mashed Potatoes. We insert herbs under the skin or inject marinades into the flesh before roasting. As leader of the Kitchen, I set a pace others will follow. I started to step out of the box by serving Korean BBQ to the ladies luncheon events. At golf events, I plated up Caribbean Jerk Chicken grilled and chopped tableside. For our Indian members and others with adventurous palates, we serve Moroccan Tagine, Mediterranean Mezas, Samosas, Vindaloos, Curries and Chutneys.

An old friend recently asked: "Patrick, why are you still going to school? You could easily write a cook book, teach and enjoy the benefits of your hard work." My answer: The more I learn, the better my skills. I don't ever foresee reaching the end of my training as a chef.

I am glad that I listened closely to Craig Goldstein at CIA way back in 1979. It has guaranteed my continued success as a chef. Today, I called Mr. Goldstein and thanked him.

N.o.t.e

- **literate** : able to use computers
- **bilingual** : (of a person) able to use two languages for communication, or (of a thing) using or involving two languages
- **heed** : to pay attention to something, especially advice or a warning
- **deploy** : to move soldiers or equipment to a place where they can be used when they are needed
- **onboard** : on a ship, train, plane or other vehicle
- **USS Baatan** : multipurpose amphibious assault ship
- **goods** : items for sale, or the things that you own
- **proctor** : someone who supervises (an examination)
- **cedar** : a tall wide evergreen tree
- **to go** : to be taken out, as restaurant food or drink
- **accreditation** : the act of granting credit or recognition (especially with respect to educational institution that maintains suitable standards)
- **crave** : desire

4. ProChef Level II Success ; Carol Murphy Clyne C.C.C.

With a dream of making a career shift from foodservice business owner to culinary instructor, I realized that I needed a solid foundation in the culinary arts. And there was never any doubt as to where I would get it—my education had to be from The Culinary Institute of America. I wanted to be a part of the best and the brightest at the forefront of influence and leadership in the culinary profession.

Before coming to the CIA, I had a very successful company, Clyne &Murphy, Inc., which grew from a small corner store to a café and catering business synonymous with quality, consistency, and reliability. As a team, my husband (the Clyne) and I (the Murphy) never lost sight of our company's motto, “your personal caterers.” I handled the staffing, training, and food preparation, and my husband was responsible for the accounting and purchasing. We did this with liberal arts degrees and no formal business or culinary education. With each experience and success, we incorporated what we learned into preparing for the next one. After selling Clyne &Murphy in September 2004, I was ready to apply the practical knowledge I had gained over the years to my next experience—ProChef Certification at the CIA.

The ProChef Certification process is intense, challenging, and rewarding. Not only did the program give me the opportunity to meet fellow students from around the world, but it also exposed me to a group of brilliant chefs and instructors, academics, and administrators—people who set the industry standard. The chef-instructors, through their lectures and hands-on training, led me to fine-tune my practical knowledge of the kitchen and develop a working knowledge of food science. The solid values, high standards, and encouragement I received enabled me to pass ProChef

Levels I and II and become a Certified Chef de Cuisine. The bar I had previously set had been raised and my passion for the craft intensified.

The passion for cooking and the sense of community at The Culinary Institute of America is palpable. It is energizing, inspiring—even addicting. And my CIA education is continuing, with classes in Mastering Wine, Culinary Communications, and Food Styling to further hone my skills and prepare me to reach ProChef Level III/Certified Executive Chef status.

By combining ProChef certification with my 20 years of business experience and my degree in Education, I'm able to realize my dream of becoming a culinary educator. Recently I was hired by Carl Schaedel and Co., Inc. to run the cooking school at the state-of-the-art Viking Culinary Center and Appliance Resource Showroom in Fairfield, New Jersey. I was also asked to join the CIA in the position of visiting instructor for the Food Enthusiasts program. In this role I will be teaching hands-on classes to teens using recipes that I designed independently.

I feel privileged to be part of the CIA and to be teaching young people the skills they need to integrate better food choices into their fast-paced lives. Ultimately, I hope to impart to them the same level of inspiration and encouragement that was offered to me by the CIA's chef-instructors, whose collective wisdom will continue to guide me through my newly expanding career.

N.o.t.e

- **Chef de Cuisine(C.C.C)** : A chef who is the supervisor in charge of food production in a foodservice operation. This could be a single unit of a multi-unit operation or a free-standing operation. He or she is in essence the chef of this operation with the final decision-making power as it relates to culinary operations. The person in this position must supervise a minimum of three (3) full-time people in the production of food. Normally, in larger operations, the is responsible to the executive chef and possesses a basic knowledge of food safety and sanitation, culinary nutrition, and supervisory management.
- **synonymous** : having the same meaning
- **liberal arts** : studies intended to provide general knowledge and intellectual skills (rather than occupational or professional skills)
- **incorporate** : to include something as part of something larger
- **palpable** : so obvious that it can easily be seen or known, or (of a feeling) so strong that it seems as if it can be touched or physically felt
- **Culinary Communications** : It is a specialist marketing communications consultancy focused on providing high level communications support to various food and beverage operations and related companies.
- **state-of-the-art** : the highest level of development at a particular time (especially the present time)
- **Enthusiast** : a person who is very interested in and involved with a particular subject or activity

R.e.f.e.r.n.c.e.s

http://www.ciaprochef.com/distance/prochef/success_judy.html

http://dictionary.cambridge.org/

http://encarta.msn.com/encnet/features/dictionary/

http://en.wikipedia.org/wiki/

http://www.onelook.com/

http://www.merriam-webster.com/

http://www.chefabroad.com/content/view/150/60/

http://www.pkh.com.sg/divisions/hc/index.htm

Chapter 21 Introduction to Certified Master Chef

This chapter introduces some facts about Certified Master Chef of the United States of America. Also Certified Master Chef Examination Manual by American Culinary Federation is added at the end of this book.

The Certified Master Chef status is coveted enviously by some of the best chefs in the world. It is also the ultimate goal of many culinary graduates. What makes it the highest accolade for a chef?

The title of a Certified Master Chef has been awarded in Europe for more than half a century. To date, thousands of certificates have been given. In America, however, it was started in 1981 by the American Culinary Federation (ACF), a very recent phenomena by anyone's standard.

The Certified Master Chef level is the highest and most demanding level of achievement of all the certification levels presented by the ACF. Many say it is even more demanding than the European equivalent because it takes into account the need to grasp regional and international cuisine, and not merely classical cuisine techniques.

It is an extremely stressful process that can require months of study even for the best and brightest among us. Michael Ruhman describes the entire process in his seminal book, The Soul of a Chef: The Journey Toward Perfection.

- How many ACF Certified Master Chefs are there?

In 1981, only 5 master chefs certifications were awarded. As of February 2005, there are 59 certified master chefs.

- Who recognizes the certification?

Besides the ACF, the certification is also recognized by the World Association of Cooks Societies.

- Where is the certification exam held?

There are two approved test sites: The Culinary Institute of America in Hyde Park, N.Y., and Greystone, the CIA's West Coast campus in Napa Valley, Calif.

- What is the exam like?

All candidates must pass an intensive 10-day test of culinary skills and knowledge. The day starts at 7 a.m. and ends late in the evening at 9 p.m. They are judged by a panel of Certified Master Chefs and Certified Master Pastry Chefs. Topics include:

Food Safety and Sanitation

Nutrition

Hospitality supervision

American, International, Classical cuisine

Bakery / pastry / patisserie

Dietary cooking/nutrition

Menu development

Supervisory Management

- How much does it cost?

The tuition fee is US$3,000. However, candidates should also budget for travel, accommodation and housing. The entire exam can cost as much as US$6,000.

- What are the benefits of being a certified master chef?

The main benefit is really self-satisfaction—to put yourself through the test is to challenge yourself and know that all your years of hard work, experience, skill and knowledge add up to something important. The honour comes later along with the possible job offers and publicity.

- What are the responsibilities of a certified master chef?

First and foremost, to uphold the highest standards of culinary arts in every way. From the constant improvement of skill and knowledge, to guiding other young chefs on their path to becoming great chefs.

N.o.t.e

- **covet** : to desire something strongly, especially something which belongs to someone else
- **accolade** : praise and approval
- **the World Association of Cooks Societies** : The World Association of Chefs' Societies, or WACS in short, is a global network of chefs associations first founded in October 1928 at the Sorbonne in Paris. At that first congress there were 65 delegates from 17 countries, representing 36 national and international associations, and the venerable August Escoffier was named the first Honourary President of WACS. Today, this global body has 72 official chefs associations as members, with three that just joined at the 31st World Congress in March. The biennel congress is a hallmark tradition of WACS and has been organised in over 20 cities across the world throughout its illustrious 74-year history, WACS is managed by an elected presidential body consisting of the WACS president, vice president, treasurer, secretary general and ambassador honourary president, as well as a board of continenal directors that look after the regions of Asia, Europe, Africa, the Pacific and the Americas. A separate committee manages all culinary competition-related affairs. Relevant details can be found in the Who's Who (link) page of this website.

R.e.f.e.r.n.c.e.s

http://dictionary.cambridge.org/

http://encarta.msn.com/encnet/features/dictionary/

http://en.wikipedia.org/wiki/

http://www.onelook.com/

http://www.merriam-webster.com/

http://www.chefabroad.com/content/view/150/60/

http://www.acfchefs.org/

http://www.wacs2000.org/index.php

Chapter 22 A Success Story of a Chef

This brief article is about Dr. Ryan who is President of The Culinary Institute of America (CIA) right now. At the age of 26 he became the youngest chef ever to achieve Certified Master Chef (C.M.C.) status from the America Culinary Federation (ACF).

1. President Ryan's Biography

Dr. Ryan is the fifth President of The Culinary Institute of America (CIA), having assumed the presidency on November 1, 2001. A 1977 graduate of the CIA, Chef Ryan is the first alumnus and first faculty member to rise through the ranks to President.

Prior to becoming college president, Dr. Ryan was the CIA's Executive Vice President. His responsibilities in this role included supervision of all of the college's degree programs and continuing education, the CIA's intellectual properties, a 72,000-volume library, food and beverage operations, career services, and institutional research.

President Ryan has been instrumental in generating the sustained growth, innovation, and quality improvements that have shaped the CIA. After working as a chef in the restaurant industry, he returned to his alma mater in 1982 to serve on the faculty. As part of the team that developed the CIA's American Bounty Restaurant, Dr. Ryan was a leader in the American cuisine movement. Under his direction, the college launched several new programs, including the world's first bachelor's degree programs in culinary arts management and baking and pastry arts management; developed a highly successful publishing program; fashioned award-winning videos and television shows; dramatically expanded the college's continuing education programs; and strengthened an already gifted faculty.

A native of Pittsburgh, Dr. Ryan holds the distinction of being the youngest national president of the America Culinary Federation (ACF) and, at the time, the youngest chef ever to achieve Certified Master Chef (C.M.C.) status from that organization. He also served as ACF vice president and chairman and is a former chairman of the editorial council for their publication, The National Culinary Review. President Ryan was named the ACF's 1998 Chef of the Year and is one of five Americans ever to receive the Presidential Medal from the World Association of Cooks Societies. He also captained the U.S. Culinary Olympic Team to a world championship.

Tim Ryan earned his doctorate degree in education from The University of Pennsylvania and bachelor's and Master of Business Administration (M.B.A.) degrees from the University of New Haven.

2. President Ryan's Career Snapshot

1977 graduate of The Culinary Institute of America, Tim Ryan, 47, is the first alumnus and the first faculty member to rise through the ranks to become the college's fifth President

After working as a chef in the restaurant industry, President Ryan returned to CIA in 1982. Dr. Ryan has been instrumental in strengthening and enhancing the college by :

Launching the world's first bachelor's degree programs in Culinary Arts Management and Baking and Pastry Arts Management;

Developing a highly successful publishing program;

Fashioning award-winning videos and television shows;

Expanding the college's continuing education programs;

Developing the American Bounty Restaurant ; and

Strengthening an already gifted faculty roster

Dr. Ryan holds the distinction of being the youngest national president of the American Culinary Federation (ACF), elected at age 36.

At age 26, Tim Ryan became the youngest person ever to earn Certified Master Chef (C.M.C.) status from the ACF.

President Ryan has served as ACF vice president and chairman, and is a former chairman of the editorial council for the ACF's publication, The National Culinary Review.

Tim Ryan was named the ACF's Chef of the Year and is one of five Americans ever to receive the Presidential Medal from the World Association of Cooks Societies, in 1998.

Dr. Ryan has won numerous Gold Medals in international competitions throughout his career, including four Gold Medals and the World Championship at the 1984 and 1988 Culinary Olympics in Germany.

President Ryan has produced a host of successful culinary books which are all James Beard Award nominees, including The New Professional Chef, Techniques of Healthy Cooking, and An American Bounty.

A native of Pittsburgh, Dr. Ryan earned his doctorate degree in education from The University of Pennsylvania and bachelor's and Master of Business Administration (M.B.A.) degrees from the University of New Haven.

N.o.t.e

- **presidency** : the tenure of a president
- **alumnus(plural alumni)** : someone who has left a school, college or university after completing their studies there
- **instrumental** : serving or acting as a means or aid
- **roster** : a list of people's names, often with the jobs they have been given to do
- **James Beard Award** : Since 1986, the James Beard Foundation has been at the forefront of America's culinary revolution. The Foundation was established that year in honor of James Beard, the late cooking teacher, journalist, and food consultant who is widely considered the father of American gastronomy. The Foundation's mission is to celebrate, preserve, and nurture America's culinary heritage and diversity in order to elevate the appreciation of our culinary excellence.
  Almost every day, chefs from America's finest restaurants and hotels cook in the kitchen of James Beard's legendary Greenwich Village home, presenting their culinary art to Beard Foundation members, friends, and press in much the same way musicians perform in Carnegie Hall. For chefs, an evening at the James Beard House has all the excitement of an opening night.
  In addition to showcasing culinary artists, the Foundation offers tastings, lectures, workshops, food-related art exhibits, and educational opportunities for children. A scholarship program enables students to pursue careers in the culinary arts. The James Beard House also serves as a meeting place for other culinary organizations. The James Beard Foundation Awards, held each spring, honor professionals in the food and beverage industry for their achievements. The Awards are the culinary industry's most prestigious recognition program, generating attention throughout the nation.
- **nominee** : somebody who has been proposed for a position, honor, or office

R.e.f.e.r.n.c.e.s

http://www.ciachef.edu/media/presskit/bio.asp#bio

http://www.acfchefs.org/

http://www.jamesbeard.org/about/history.shtml

http://www.wacs2000.org/index.php

http://www.pkh.com.sg/divisions/hc/index.htm

http://dictionary.cambridge.org/

http://encarta.msn.com/encnet/features/dictionary/

http://en.wikipedia.org/wiki/

http://www.onelook.com/

http://www.merriam-webster.com/

Guide to
Kitchen Enlgish

Appendix

Guide to Kitchen English

Appendix

아래의 공인조리기능장 시험매뉴얼은 미국조리연맹이 공표한 공식내용이다. 편저자가 'Guide to Kitchen English' 를 집필하기 위한 자료 수집과정에서 인터넷에서 입수하였다. 독자들은 아래의 매뉴얼을 읽고 미국의 공인조리기능장(C.M.C.)과 한국의 조리명장 및 조리기능장 제도를 비교해보자. 조리기능이 뛰어난 조리기능장을 어떻게 선발하고 이들에게 가장 어울리는 보다 명예롭고 영속성 있는 타이틀이 무엇일까를 반드시 생각해보기 바란다. 이런 과정이 있어야 대한민국의 조리분야가 세계 속에서 한층 위상을 발휘하게 될 것이며, 조리사들뿐만 아니라 일반인들도 조리기능장이라는 타이틀을 존귀하게 생각할 것이다.

Certified Master Chef Examination Manual

by American Culinary Federation(ACF.)

The American Culinary Federation (ACF), the premier certifying body for American chefs, is pleased that you have decided to embark on the journey to validate your skills at the pinnacle of culinary certification—Certified Master Chef (CMC). The purpose of this practical exam is to verify the mastery of cooking skills of each candidate and ensure that the candidate demonstrates the utmost professionalism.

CMC exam candidates are expected to have exemplary organizational, sanitation, mentoring and cookery skills. Every aspect of this exam is designed to verify those skills, and candidates are evaluated from the time of arrival until the kitchen is clean on the final day. It is the American Culinary Federation's greatest wish for your success and that upon completion you will be one of the elite CMCs in the world.

It is your responsibility to read and understand the contents of this manual before applying for the examination. This manual contains current information about the certification examination developed by the CMC committee as of May 2006, thereby nullifying all prior publications.

All correspondence should be directed to the national headquarters of the American Culinary Federation at the following address including: address changes, handbook requests, information about the development and administration of the CMC practical examination, certification programs and recertification:

1. Application Process

General Qualification Guidelines

- Possess the practiced skills to perform culinary art to the highest standards.
- Have a foundation of quality experience and education in advanced level courses, externships and/or competitions.
- Be physically and mentally prepared to perform eight days under extreme pressure.
- Secure funding to cover expenses: application fee, examination fee, travel, housing, meals and miscellaneous based at approximately $4,000 - $6,000.

Specific Experience Requirements

- Level of practice documentation of a Certified Executive Chef (CEC) or Certified Executive Pasty Chef (CEPC) in good standing.
- Letters from two CMCs recommending the candidate for the exam.

Specific Education Requirements

The following must be completed within the past five years. The ACF's Certified Culinary Administrator (CCA) exam will be accepted as an equivalency for Management and Cost Management coursework.

- Sanitation and food safety: current sanitation certificate or Hazard Analysis and Critical Control Point (HACCP) certification.
- Cost Management: approved course completion (classroom hours or credit transfer).
- Management: approved course completion (classroom hours or credit transfer).
- Wine: approved course completion or successful completion of a 30-hour wine course from an accredited institution.

2. Application Steps

Step 1

Submit a letter of intent and the completed application to apply for the ACF Certified Master Chef Exam, along with letters of recommendation from two CMCs and the nonrefundable application fee of $300 to:

American Culinary Federation
180 Center Place Way
St. Augustine, FL 32095

Candidates will receive a copy of the Certified Master Chef Manual, be listed as a preparatory candidate and will be notified of each occurring exam for the following three terms.

Step 2

Upon receipt of the completed application and required documentation, the candidate

will receive confirmation of receipt and the exam date, as well as their status being

updated to an active candidate. From this point forward, the candidate will be subject to all policies and procedures regarding the exam.

Step 3

The last step is to register for a CMC examination. Active candidates are notified by mail of pending test dates. In addition, examination dates are listed in The National Culinary Review, the ACF's flagship publication. There must be a minimum of six active candidates enrolled for a particular date in order for the exam to be held. Presently, ACF administers one test a year usually between January and April.

Fees, Payments, Refunds and Other Expenses

Once a candidate has committed to an exam date they are to respond to the notice and follow the payment schedule as listed below.

The examination fee for the Certified Master Chef or Certified Master Pastry Chef is $3,300 (subject to change). The application fee of $300 is nonrefundable and entitles the candidate to be listed as a preparatory candidate for the next three exams.

Three months prior to the start of the exam, the candidate is required to make a deposit of $1,000.

Three weeks prior to the exam, the candidate is required to pay the remaining balance of $2,000.

Candidates accepted for an exam date, but who are unable to attend, must submit a written letter of withdrawal. Letters of withdrawal received one month prior to administration of the exam may be fully refunded. However, notices received after this time only qualify for a 75 percent refund. There will be no refunds once the exam has begun.

All other expenses associated with taking the exam (travel, room, board and etc.) are the responsibility of the candidate. This includes any charges required by the host institution for make-up exams.

3. Examination Site

The host institution conducting the examination has been carefully selected by the ACF Certification Committee in accordance with ACF standards. The host site will provide assistance to candidates to find reasonably priced room accommodations.

Facility

The building classrooms, kitchen laboratory and other instructional and examination areas have been deemed safe and meet all industry standards, as well as local codes for sanitation, health, fire and insurance. The test kitchen, classroom and examiner's room will be available for the duration of the eight-day exam.

Kitchen Laboratory

The Kitchen Laboratory contains between six and no more than 12 fully equipped individual testing stations. In addition to the individual test stations, the kitchen has already met the following requirements:

- Open gas ranges.
- General refrigerator and freezer space.

- Small equipment in excellent working condition for each station.
- Community utensils and equipment.
- Observation windows on at least one side.
- Easily controlled entrances and exits.

Small Equipment and utensils provided at each station include:

- Bain marie with whips and spoons.
- Cutting board.
- Ladles in two, four, six, eight and 12 ounces.
- China cap.
- Chinois.
- Spider.
- Skimmer.
- Food processor.
- Electric mixer.
- Scales.

Common community areas within the kitchen have the following equipment and utensils:

- Slicer.
- Blender.
- Pasta machine.
- Grinder.
- Ice cream freezer.
- Assorted pots, roasting pans, sheet pans and bowls.
- Cheesecloth, aluminum foil and plastic wrap.

Service equipment in the same pattern, sizes and color available to all candidates include :

- Large silver platter with the capacity to hold eight portions.

- Large china platter with the capacity to hold six portions.
- Assorted terrines and underliners with the capacity to hold six portions.
- Soup cups with underliners.
- Soup bowls with underliners.
- Appetizer and salad plates approximately $10\frac{1}{4}$" .
- Dinner plates $12\frac{1}{2}$" .
- Sauce boats.

One student apprentice will be available to each candidate for each kitchen laboratory segment of the entire examination. The host institution will attempt to provide each candidate with one student apprentice to remain with them for the duration of the examination, however this is not guaranteed.

Classroom and Examiner' s Room

Classroom space is provided for lectures and individual written testing. The examiner's room should be located next to the kitchen laboratory.

Resource Center

The host institution's culinary arts and hospitality management library, computers and related software, as well as audio and video equipment, will be made available to candidates.

Par Stock Items

The following is a sampling of products that should be available for use by the candidates. During the exam, any items needed by a candidate at any time must be requisitioned up to and including those on the following list. Seasonality will affect availability and should be taken into consideration by candidates.

Staples

Cornmeal
Cornstarch
Rice flour
A.P. flour
Bread flour
Carolina rice

Groceries

Olive Oil
Vegetable Oil
Peanut Oil
Vinegar(assorted)
Dajon mustard
Romato paste apurée
Tomatoes(canned)
Tabasco sauce

Srocks

White
Chicken
Brown

Produce

Shallots
Garlic
Yellow and Red Onions
Carrots
Celery
Lemons

Wines and Alcohol

Dry sherry
Dry vermout
Grand Marnier
Madeira
Port
Brandy
Standard Brandy
Standard Chablis
Red wine
Beer
Applejack
Bourbon

Cheeses

Cream cheese
Swiss/Gruyère
Parmesan type cheese
Cheddar

Dairy

Milk
Butter(unsalted)
Eggs
Skim Milk
Heavy Cream
Sour Cream
Plain Yogurth

Sauces/Misellaneous

Brown sauce
Clace de viande

Requisition and Other Supply Guidelines

The candidate is responsible for ensuring all food supplies are ordered and have arrived

within the first hour of the preparation window. If the food supplies have not arrived, it is the responsibility of the candidate to inform the kitchen proctor.

China, glass and other items must be secured by the candidate by requisition within two hours of the service window. If any items are not available that are needed, it is the responsibility of the candidate to inform the kitchen proctor.

4. Examination Schedule Overview

The order of the lectures, tests and the start and stop times may vary depending on the host institution. However, candidates must complete each segment within the designated time limit.

Wednesday prior to test start day

- Receive protein for Healthy Cooking segment ; This will be sent to the candidate's email address at 9 a.m. on the Wednesday prior to the start of the exam, unless other arrangements are made in writing to the exam coordinator two weeks prior.

Thursday prior to test start day

- Return nutritional analysis, menu and ingredient list within 24 hours ; All required information must be delivered electronically or by fax before 9 a.m. that Thursday morning. The nutritional analysis must be documented by a registered dietitian, and it will be reviewed by the CMC exam administrator for verification.

Friday

- Orientation 2 Hours
    - Draw Buffet Catering Proteins
    - Healthy Cooking Orientation

Saturday

- Storeroom Visit for Buffet Catering Supplies ········ 1 Hour
- Healthy Cooking ·· 5 Hours

Sunday

- Buffet Catering Prep ······························ 12 Hours
    - Draw Classical Cuisine Proteins

Monday

- Submit Classical Menu
- Buffet Catering Plating and Service ··········· 3 Hours
    - Draw Freestyle Cooking Protein

Tuesday

- Submit Freestyle Menu

Tuesday continued

- Classical Cuisine ······························ 4 Hours
    - Three Courses – menu items are chosen by candidate

Wednesday

- Freestyle Cooking ······························ 4 Hours
    - Four Courses – one course must be non-meat, fish or poultry
- Draw Global Cuisine Menu

Thursday

- Global Cuisine ······························ 4 Hours

o Three entrees

Friday

- Baking and Pastry ………………………………………………… 5 Hours
  - Draw Continental Cuisine Menu

Saturday

- Continental Cuisine – morning …………………………… 4 Hours
  - Three Entrees
- Market Basket – afternoon ………………………………… 5 Hours
  - Five Courses

Note: A 30-minute service window is applied to the end of each time frame, except for baking and pastry, and buffet catering.

5. Master Chef Examination Outline

Over the eight days of the CMC examination, the tests are administered in eight major segments.

1. Healthy Cooking
2. Buffet Catering
3. Classical Cuisine
4. Freestyle Cooking
5. Global Cuisine

6. Baking and Pastry
7. Continental and Northern Europe Cuisines
8. Market Basket

Grading Criteria and Procedures

There are eight major categories in the eight-day master chef examination. Each segment of the examination is graded in two parts:

- Kitchen Skills ; maximum 100 points and weighted to reflect 35 points of final grade.

- Presentation and Tasting ; maximum 100 points and weighted to reflect 65 points of final grade.

A perfect score is 100 points and a minimum passing score is 70 points. The minimum passing final cumulative score is 75 points.

Since each scoring segment can have one to five judges, a candidate's grade is determined by the average of the judge's scores. The minimum passing score (the combined average of the kitchen skill, and presentation and tasting scores) for each segment is 70 points.

A candidate must have a cumulative passing score of 75 percent during the first 7 days of the exam in order to participate in the last day of the exam.

A candidate may continue with the examination even if they fail one segment, but must maintain a cumulative average of 75 percent. The failure of two segments (less than 70 points) results in an automatic withdrawal from the examination.

The candidate may be permitted to retake any major failed. All retakes will be administered at the next CMC exam and availability is subject to the host institution. Candidates retaking tests do so at their own expense and fees as determined by the host institution and are payable to the institution.

Candidates who fail a segment after taking it for the third time have failed the entire exam and may not retake the individual test segments.

Instead must reapply for the full eight-day examination.

The Final – Day 8

The final segment administered on the eighth day counts for 35 percent of the total

grade. It consists of two tests, Continental Cuisine/Northern Europe and Market Basket. The minimum passing grade for either test is 70 points and the combined average score of the two tests must equal or exceed 75 points. A score of less than 70 points on either segment of the final will result in a failure, regardless of the combined average score.

Candidates who fail one major and the final have failed the entire Certified Master Chef/Certified Master Pastry Chef Examination. They may not retake the individual test segments, but instead must reapply for the full eight-day examination.

Candidates who pass the six major tests and then fail the final can retake the final within two years or two exams (in case of cancellation one year). If the candidate fails to retake the final (either the first part, second part or the full day) within two years or two exams, their test scores are null and void, and they must reapply for the entire eight-day examination.

Score sheets are subject to change based on test requirements.

6. CMC Exam Majors

1) Healthy Cooking

Briefing : One hour and 30 minutes, including written exam.

Time format : Four hours and 30 minutes kitchen preparation, and 30 minutes service.

Objective : The candidate must demonstrate knowledge of Healthy Cooking principles through the development and preparation of a four-course meal for 10 people. The objective is to be met through the preparation of the meal in accordance with sound nutritional principles, a balanced focus, portion size, and the use of added salt, fats and sugar. The mastery of cooking principles will be assessed in the formulation of the menu and its components.

Demonstrated competencies

- Four classical cuts.
- Four cooking methods.
- Knowledge of platter service.

Activities

At 9 a.m. on the Wednesday prior to the start of the CMC exam, each candidate will receive a market basket ingredients list containing:

- Three protein items (appropriate combination of meat, fish and poultry).
- One grain.
- Three fruits.
- Lettuce.

A nutritional analysis, verified by registered dietitian, of a four-course menu and the appropriate food requisitions must be submitted to the CMC exam administrator no later than 9 a.m. on the Thursday prior to the start of CMC exam. The exam coordinator can provide contact resources for registered dietitians upon request.

The menu must consist of the following courses:

- Appetizer, served hot.
- Salad.
- Main course.
- Dessert, served hot, cold or any combination.

The total caloric value of the meal should not exceed 1000 kcal. The balance should be 15-20 percent protein, 45-60 percent carbohydrates and 25-30 percent fat.

The candidate will be given one hour and 30 minutes of classroom time to complete the nutritional component of the exam, four hours and 30 minutes for preparation, and thirty minutes for serving. The meal will be served in the 30-minute window at the end of the preparation time frame in the following manner: four portions plated for individual service and six portions on platters for Russian service.

Grading and Testing Criteria

- Serving method and presentation, 15 percent.
- Cooking fundamentals, 15 percent.
- Ingredient compatibility, 15 percent.
- Portion size and nutritional guidelines, 15 percent.
- Taste, 40 percent.

Buffet Catering

Briefing : One hour.

Time format : 12 hours preparation, and three hours setup and presentation time.

Objective : The candidate must demonstrate knowledge of the different types of garde manger products, their make-up and preparation procedures. The candidate should demonstrate an understanding of the functionality of the garde manger kitchen and the utilitarian philosophies attached to it. The candidate will also demonstrate the high art form attributes of presentation that is necessary in a cold food competition.

Demonstrated competencies

- Emulsified forcemeat.
- Product utilization as related to the garde manger kitchen.
- Cured protein.
- Cold salad.
- Two standing garnishes.
- Platter poured with chemise and aspic may be reinforced with gelatin, but must be of appropriate flavor and color.

- Cold mousse.
- Appropriate sauce.

Activities

- The candidate will receive the assignment and they have 12 hours to submit a written requisition for required materials.

- Candidates are allowed to bring their own platter for presentation, however, only the host facility china may be used for plating.

- A cold main course that would be served during a special festivity will be prepared, therefore fulfilling the demonstrated competency section. The candidate will prepare cold buffet items to be served in the following manner: four portions plated and eight portions on a platter as served on a buffet.

Assignment Format

The candidate will receive an assignment including the items listed below. Some of each item must be used to avoid point removal. All other supporting ingredients to be used must be requisitioned by the candidate during the storeroom visit on the first day.

- Two primary protein items.
- One secondary protein item.
- Two vegetable items.
- One starch based item.
- One supplementary item.

Grading and Testing Criteria

- Serving method and presentation, 20 percent.
- Cooking fundamentals, 15 percent.
- Ingredient compatibility and portion size, 10 percent.
- Competencies, 15 percent.
- Taste, 40 percent.

Classical Cuisine

Briefing : One hour.
Time format : Four hours preparation and 30-minute service window.

Objective : The candidate must demonstrate the ability to understand, interpret and execute the philosophy of Auguste Escoffier and classical cuisine as prescribed in the Le Guide Culinaire. The candidate will demonstrate a thorough knowledge of the foundations of classical cuisine and preparation throughout the presented menu. The mastery of classical techniques and presentation will be strictly adhered to according to Le Guide Culinaire.

Activities

- Draw protein items at the end of the second day of the CMC exam.
- Develop a menu using recipes from Le Guide Culinaire, The Complete Guide to the Art of Modern Cooking by Auguste Escoffier.
- Consommé selection will be given during protein drawing and the consommé may be derived from available stocks. The preparation of a white bouillon is not required, although it is reasonable to impose the same flavor profile incurred when a white bouillon is used.
- Submit a menu and shopping list at the start of the third day of the CMC exam.
- Receive storeroom supplies.
- The candidate must prepare 10 portions and platters are to be appropriate for Russian service :
    - Soup – four plated portions and six portions in a soup terrine.
    - Fish course – four plated portions and six portions on a restaurant platter, and both must be served with the applicable accompaniments.
    - Entrée – four plated portions and six portions on a restaurant

platter, and both must be served with the applicable accompaniments.

Grading and Testing Criteria

- Classical serving method, 15 percent.
- Classical presentation, 20 percent.
- Classical cooking methodology, 20 percent.
- Portion size, 5 percent.
- Taste, 40 percent.

2) Freestyle

Briefing: One hour.

Time format: Four hours production and 30-minute service window.

Objective: To verify the mastery of a candidate's skills in relation to the construction and preparation of a menu. This segment of the exam should demonstrate the candidate's personal cooking style and philosophy through all aspects of the menu. The judging team will assess the performance reflected through the mastery of all standard cooking fundamentals and menu methodology as a basis for evaluation.

Activities

The candidate will receive a market basket at the close of the buffet presentation. The supporting ingredients must be requisitioned by noon the following day.

- Six protein items.
- Four vegetable items.

- Three starch items.
- Lettuce.
- Three supplementary items.

Menu Requirements

Each ingredient in the basket must be used to some extent. A written requisition for supplemental ingredients must be submitted within one hour to the proctor and delivery can be expected within one hour. A four course menu must be submitted within 30 minutes from the candidate's start time to the proctor. The menu will be presented as four plated portions and six portions appropriate for Russian service.

The four courses will be comprised of the following selection:

- Appetizer or soup.
- Fish course.
- Salad.
- Main course.

Grading/Testing Criteria

- Serving method and portion size, 15 percent.
- Cooking fundamentals, 15 percent.
- Menu composition, 15 percent.
- Presentation, 15 percent.
- Taste, 40 percent.

3) Global Cuisine

Briefing: One hour.

Time format: Four hours preparation and 30 minutes service.

Objective: The candidate must demonstrate knowledge of several global cuisines. The practical component of this discipline will be demonstrated by the preparation of three main dishes from three different regions of the world. It is expected that the candidate demonstrate a knowledge representative of the traditions, philosophies and methodology that is indicative of each cuisine. The methods of service and preparation should directly relate to the traditional integrity of the dish, and demonstrate a mastery of the same by presenting the dishes in the style of a special occasion for that cuisine.

Main Areas of Testing

- Cuisines of the Americas.
- Cuisines of Asia.
- Cuisines the Mediterranean.

Activities

The candidate will draw an assignment the day before the test and will requisition all ingredients needed for preparation of the assignment. Platters are to be appropriate for Russian service.

The candidate will prepare 10 portions of each region's main dish:

- Main dish one ; four plated portions and six portions in the appropriate serving dish.

- Main dish two ; four plated portions and six portions in the appropriate serving dish.

- Main dish three ; four plated portions and six portions in the appropriate serving dish.

Grading and Testing Criteria

- Serving method and portion size, 15 percent.
- Cooking fundamentals, 15 percent.
- Presentation, 15 percent.
- Adherence to global cuisine's principals, 15 percent.
- Taste, 40 percent.

4) Baking & Pastry

Briefing: One hour.

Time format: Five hours preparation and finishing

Objective: To verify the candidate's knowledge and preparation of the mandated competencies listed below. The purpose of this segment is to demonstrate that the candidate is well versed in baking and pastry skills and is competent in the production of the same. Special attention should be paid to the product consistency and detail of the finishing techniques, such as product shape, baking doneness, size consistency and marketability.

Activities

The candidate will prepare 10 portions of a hot or cold kitchen dessert that should include the five fundamental components of a complete dessert. This should be presented for tasting.

- One, two-pound recipe of a yeast leavened product per the candidate's choice.
- Two dozen portions of a chemically leavened quick bread product per the candidate's choice.

- Two dozen portions of a puff pastry vol-au-vent or bouchée. The puff pastry will be provided by the proctor.

Grading/Testing Criteria

- Product size and shape consistency, 15 percent.
- Presentation finishing techniques, 15 percent.
- Baking techniques fundamentals, 15 percent.
- Marketability, 15 percent.
- Taste and texture, 40 percent.

5) Continental and Northern Europe Cuisines

Briefing : One hour.

Time format: Four hours preparation and 30 minutes presentation.

Objective: The candidate must demonstrate knowledge of Continental and Northern Europe Cuisines. The practical component of this discipline will be demonstrated by the preparation of three main dishes from three of the countries of this region. It is expected that the candidate be able to demonstrate a knowledge representative of the traditions, philosophies and methodology indicative of each cuisine. The methods of service and preparation should directly relate to the traditional integrity of the dish, and demonstrate a mastery of the same by presenting the dishes in the style of a special occasion for that cuisine.

The areas of testing are:

- Cuisines of Spain and Portugal.
- Cuisines of Germany, Austria and The Netherlands.
- Cuisines of Switzerland.
- Cuisines of Italy.

- Cuisines of Russia and Poland.
- Cuisines of England and Scotland.
- Cuisines of Scandinavia.

Activities

The candidate will draw an assignment the day before the test and will requisition all ingredients needed for preparation of the assignment. Platters are to be appropriate for Russian service.

The candidate will prepare 10 portions of each course:

- Main dish one ; four plated portions and six portions in the appropriate serving dish.

- Main dish two ; four plated portions and six portions in the appropriate serving dish.

- Main dish three ; four plated portions and six portions in the appropriate serving dish.

Grading and Testing Criteria

- Serving method and portion size, 15 percent.
- Cooking fundamentals, 15 percent.
- Presentation, 15 percent.
- Adherence to international cuisine principals, 15 percent.
- Taste, 40 percent.

6) Market Basket

Time format: Five hours preparation and 30 minutes service.

Objective: To evaluate the candidate's ability to write and prepare a menu within specific time constraints at the highest level by demonstrating the mastery of all culinary foundational skills. All kitchen activities will be thoroughly scrutinized and evaluated with the prescribed mastery in mind. It is fully expected that a mastery of cooking methodology, butchery and craftsmanship will be demonstrated during the cooking period. Furthermore, the end result will be expected to exemplify these standards to the fullest extent of plating, platter construction, taste and finishing skills.

Activities

The candidate will be presented with a market basket and each ingredient in the basket must be used to some extent. A written requisition for supplemental ingredients must be submitted within one hour to the proctor and delivery can be expected within one hour. A five-course menu must be submitted within 30 minutes from the candidate's start time to the proctor and it must be presented as four plated portions and six portions for platter service.

The market basket will contain the following ingredients:

- Three seafood proteins.
- Three other proteins.
- Nine vegetable items.
- Four starch based items.
- One fruit.
- Lettuce.
- One legume.

The five courses will be comprised in the following manner:

- Appetizer.
- Soup.
- Fish course.
- Salad.
- Main course.

Grading and Testing Criteria

- Serving method and portion size, 15 percent.
- Cooking fundamentals, 15 percent.
- Ingredient compatibility, 15 percent.
- Presentation, 15 percent.
- Taste, 40 percent.

source :

http://www.acfchefs.org/download/documents/certify/CMC_Exam_Manual.pdf

저 / 자 / 소 / 개

강경재(姜炅宰)

- 전북대학교 졸업(학사)
- 호원대학교 졸업(학사)
- 경기대학교 대학원 관광경영학과 졸업(경영학 석사)
- 경기대학교 대학원 관광경영학과 졸업(경영학 박사)
- 전 군산 미공군기지 제8헌병대대 언어전문관
- 전 경기대학교, 호원대학교, 남서울대학교, 혜전대학, 혜천대학, 군장공업대학, 원광보건대학 강사
- 전 혜전대학 호텔조리계열 학부장
- 전 혜전대학 호텔조리외식계열 계열장
- 전 혜전대학 호텔조리외식계열 음료경영전공 전공장
- 현 혜전대학 호텔조리외식계열 일식전공 전공장

[저서 및 논문]

- 신관광영어강독, 학문사(1998)
- Hotel & Food Service Cuisine English, 백산출판사(1999)
- Guide to the Student Chef, 대왕사(2001)
- Guide to Culinary English, 대왕사(2003)
- Guide to Food Styling English, 대왕사(2005)
- Guide to Recipe for the Student Chef, 대왕사(2006)
- Guide to Culinary and Foodservice English, LBH(2007)
- Guide to Recipes of Oriental Cuisines, 대왕사(2009)
- Guide to the Culinary Industry, 백산출판사(2010)
- 「호텔 레스토랑의 데이터베이스 마케팅에 관한 연구」 외 다수

Guide to Kitchen English

2008년 3월 5일 초판 1쇄 발행
2014년 8월 20일 초판 3쇄 발행

저 자 강 경 재
발행인 진 욱 상 · 진 성 원

발행처 백산출판사

서울시 성북구 정릉로 157(백산빌딩 4층)
등 록 : 1974. 1. 9. 제 1-72호
전 화 : 914-1621, 917-6240
FAX : 912-4438
http://www.ibaeksan.kr
editbsp@naver.com

값 13,000원

ISBN 978-89-6183-043-0